FINDING
THE POLLYANNA ZONE

Garry Isaacs

CONTENTS

INTRODUCTION

Chemicals, pharmaceuticals and air pollution are killing people or at least making them sick. Pollution is everywhere, worldwide. Although the most dreaded disease, cancer is still not well understood, it is now becoming recognized by the medical community and the public that radiation and chemicals are playing a big role in its incidence and not enough in its abatement. One has to wonder what role drug manufacturers play in the promotion of chemicals and radiation instead of a cure because they would experience enormous losses if a real cure was to replace their drugs. I have had friends, young men, that have died of cancer after being careless in their application of farm chemicals. DDT was banned because of its dangerous effects on humans. Insecticides and herbicides of all kinds are a compromise at best, the public being sold on the idea that the benefits of their use outweigh the consequences and the side effects. It has become quite evident in recent years that profits are of more importance to soulless corporations than the well being of their fellow men or their customers. Everybody in the company just works there with no sense of responsibility for the outcome.

A myriad of problems need fixed and many obstacles need to be overcome before the environment can be clean and energy can be made cheap and easy for the masses. It is attainable, but not in an economy that runs on debt and the manipulations of a few power addicted money mongers and imperialists. The huge Ponzi scheme they have created to concentrate the world's wealth into their own hands must, and will crumble like all other Ponzi schemes. A lust for power and personal treasure has ruined the chances for a cleaner world but a change is coming soon. I call the change a transition and the near objective The Pollyanna Zone.

CHAPTER ONE

THE UNEASY EARTH

IT'S NOT MAGIC, IT'S SENSIBILITY

It has been said that we are what we eat. Food is essential and should be protected. In order to feed the world, food products need to be better preserved and last longer. This is the premise upon which the effort described herein originates. Making a profit in farming has become dependent upon the use of farm chemicals. Growers have been put out of business for not being able to compete because of lower yield experienced without using farm chemicals. Production and pricing of their products that are determined by the supply of disease free commodities are essential for their success. In the mean time, consumers have been forced to settle for food products that have been profusely inundated with farm chemicals that were used to increase yield, preserve them for longer terms and make them look good and appealing to the customer. Organic growers have been unable to sell their products because of losses to disease and the lesser yield for the lack of supplementary synthetic fertilizers. Conversely, the public has become more aware of these factors and more concerned for personal health. More and more consumers are willing to pay a little more for organically produced food products for the sake of being healthier and more productive, improving their lifestyles and a general sense of well being.

Traditional production methods of a lot of U.S. growers of food products are being moved over to make room for at least some organic farming. It is an expensive transition since it takes three years of non-chemical farming on a particular piece of land in order to qualify as organic with the U.S. Department of Agriculture. The land also has to be protected from the invasion of chemicals from other non-organic fields. The production of smaller organic potatoes, onions, tomatoes etc. sold in smaller packages, and for higher prices has made it economically possible for these transitions to occur. Preserving these products without chemical disinfectants is essential for longer shelf life.

The trend has been very helpful for the introduction and use of a new technology such as Humigation as an alternative to chemical disease control. New and invasive technology keeps storage air for these products clean and disease free, contributing in the long run to overall human health. It is refreshing to finally find a way to make contributions to this human need contrary to the methods forced down the throats of growers and consumers by corporate giants that drive the activities of academia and the governments of the world with power and money.

It is an ominous concept for a small company to think it can provide clean air and clean health to the entire population of the earth or to change the way energy is produced in the world. Of course it can't but as others catch on, and I believe they finally are, there will be many companies and individuals that will participate in the effort with them or beside them to make it eventually happen. People can be healthier, happier and more productive, living better lifestyles and raising healthier families with attention to technologies that really work and that are not controlled by the corporate government and academic complex that stands arrogantly in the way of truth, progress and innovation.

The economic principle of supply and demand as a natural way for economics to be stabilized, though, by itself is devoid of government or banker intervention, most often moves and adjusts too slow for comfort. The peaks are high and the valleys low and adjustment so slow that people starve and governments fail. J.P. Morgan was not the first to recognize the opportunities created by this phenomenon but he was the first one to the scene when, under Grover Cleveland's presidency in 1893, the economy of the United States fell into dire straits. As prices fell taking business profits with them, unemployment skyrocketed as workers were laid off to save the companies they worked for from total failure. The panic of 1893 created a run on gold as people began demanding an exchange of their currency for the precious metal that had been standardized to back it. The U.S. Treasury had established by statute, a minimum of $100 million in gold to be held in the treasury at all times. The run on gold brought the reserves down to $65 million by January 24, 1895 and a week later it had dropped to $45 million.

In 1893, U.S. President Grover Cleveland and his Treasury Secretary, John Carlisle desperately tried to prop up the U.S. economy by selling treasury bonds to the public in the amount of $60 million but by then the public was not confident enough to buy them in time to save the economy. The public were not the only ones in a panic. The federal government was nearly insolvent. Railroad mogul, J.P. Morgan knew that a failing economy was not going to support his railroad based empire and he was keenly aware of the problem the federal government was facing. This created both crisis and opportunity for him. So, although it was politically dangerous for Cleveland, a deal was struck whereby Morgan and his syndicate bought $100 million of U.S. Treasury bonds and paid for them in gold. the transaction propped up the economy and saved the day for the failing government economy. Morgan made $millions on the deal and, the public, not being fond of the idea of the government being involved with wall street did not re-elect Cleveland for another term.

The great depression as a result of the crash of the U.S. stock market in 1929 brought a new theory to light for short term fixing of the economy. John Maynard Keynes introduced the concept of lowering taxes on corporations and high government spending as a means of creating jobs and propping up a failing economy. The theory, known as Keynesian Economics, along with a deal with Federal Reserve bankers to provide loans to be paid by income tax created in 1913 was instated by Franklin Delano Roosevelt in 1935. The *"new deal"*, much resembled the deal made between Cleveland and Morgan in 1895. The *"new deal"* once again temporarily rescued the failing U.S. economy. This time the corporate government complex was sealed for good and the American people were plunged into a never ending indebtedness that was to grow exponentially in the new 21st century. The *"new deal"* was supported by a new tax on the incomes of Americans without their consent or approval, a tax that had never before been implemented in the United States.

The panic of 1893 was not the first time bankers had gotten involved with the government and the economy. Even Meyer Amschel Rothschild who financed both sides of wars to get gain, was not the first. In fact money has controlled men and governments since the beginning of the history of governments. Such influence solidified a trend that was to prevail through the creation of the Federal Reserve in 1914 and onward to the multi-billion dollar banker bailout of 2008. Money flowed from the Federal Reserve Bank, not just as an exchange but in the same direction in two ways by then. It was not just to bail out the bankers but also to the purchase of $billions in stocks and bonds by the Federal Reserve over the following years through a program called *"quantitative easing"*.

As the stock market was propped, the national debt grew exponentially, the public became outraged, paving the way for the election of the independent Republican candidate, Donald Trump.

It felt like a 180 degree turn from the traditional establishment. Once again, trust in the Federal Government and Wall Street had been lost, this time to a more magnified degree. This was a unique situation. Trump was not beholding to the bankers nor to the rich elite that had supported and manipulated past elections. He was rich enough to finance his own campaign along with support from the American people who were fed up with dishonesty and crooked dealing between the Federal Government and Wall Street and the interference of foreign governments, prominently by the ones with oil for energy interests.

The amalgamation of governments with bankers, the insertion of corporate bureaucrats into the government with corporate special interests and the absolute dependence of mainstream academia for their support on both government and private corporate factions has created a consortium of special interest driven activity that has overshadowed the best interests of the public. It has been done by restricting the development of revolutionary ideas and devices to wealthy special interests. An understanding of how these factions developed and prevailed provides insight into the reason for the stagnation and prevention of new and better, yet invasive technologies. Nothing can be allowed from outside by the corporate, government, academic complex to interrupt or replace their long established, though antiquated habits, so they stand in the way of new technologies that tend to interfere with their own agendas.

CHAPTER TWO

GOOD IDEAS

IF IT SEEMS IMPOSSIBLE
IT MAY JUST BE BECAUSE A SOLUTION
IS YET TO BE FOUND

I was standing alone, looking out the window of the abandoned upstairs lunchroom of the 50,000 square foot former vegetable warehouse and packing plant that I had purchased from the City of Nampa, Idaho to process precious metal concentrates. I was pondering the dust that was being discharged from the equipment and the mills with the residual air. We had set up four machines that I had designed and developed for the comminution and extraction of gold from hard rock and placer ores. Each of the four mills had a discharge stack that vented the air from the comminution mills vertically through the roof of the building and into the atmosphere. It was 1984.

Particle emissions were not regulated to the point of preventing their discharge into the atmosphere at the time, at least not yet in my neighborhood. I was concerned about not only the particles settling on my roof but also concerned that I might be losing microscopic particles of precious metals that could be recovered by a better scrubber system at the back of the classifier, so, I went to work on the idea. Fred Reynolds, an old friend from the hometown in Idaho was working for me at the time. He was old enough to be my father and sometimes acted like it. I loved the guy but I couldn't afford to pay him what he was worth. Whenever something that I said or did disturbed Fred, he would say to me "*I have a headache, lets go get a cup of coffee*". And so we would go to a restaurant somewhere and talk. I knew that his service to me was temporary so I made use of his creative mind.

Over one of these "*headache....cup of coffee*" sessions I brought up that I wanted to design a scrubber to salvage the residual dust from the mill tailpipes. We brainstormed for awhile and within a day or so he came up with an idea, drawing it out on a piece of paper as he talked. The idea was to build a box to run the water and concentrates through at the same time with four paddle wheels to stir the surface of the water so the particles would be wetted on their way through the pipe. We went home and slept on the idea. We returned in the morning whereupon Fred anxiously caught me early with the words, "*Don't build it, it won't work*". I told him that I thought it would work and we were going to build it and see, so we did and it worked. How well it worked we never found out - it was never tested for efficiency or effectiveness of performance but it did stop the visual emissions on the roof, good enough for what it was for.

This experience started me thinking about emissions control. The U.S. Environmental Protection Agency was formed in 1970 by the executive order of President Richard Nixon and ratified by Congress but its regulatory tentacles had not reached us at the time of these experiments. However, there was evidence that it was growing in the influence of its enforcement arm and that it would soon cover the nation. I began thinking about how to arrest emissions from all kinds of industrial processes while struggling to keep afloat an ore processing business that was rapidly failing for lack of access to profitable ore. The business slowly failed for lack of capital and the absence of sustainable contracts.

Meanwhile, I met a man in a nearby neighborhood who had addressed the problem of industrial emissions scrubbing with steam. I recognized that the tiny droplets created by heating water to steam would have a positive effect for the collection of particulates from an airstream. I approached the man, or rather his son-in-law representative of the process and asked how much money it would take to buy the technology. His reply was a discouragingly high number, obviously taken from the dreamworld, so I drove away somewhat disappointed but still undaunted. I began to wonder how I could reduce the size of water droplets without spending the energy to create them by heat. Thus began the mental process of inventing a device that became known as a Dynamic Multi-venturi (DMV) and in agriculture, eventually named Humigator. The process to be performed by the Humigator was naturally called Humigation.

Humigation is a hybrid word derived from "*humidity*" and "*fumigation*" although fumigation is the employment of chemicals, none of which is required for Humigation. Humigator uses no filters, only water, and has since proven itself to be extremely effective for controlling the spread of pathogens by vacuuming them from the atmosphere in a room and removing and containing them into a tank of water before discharging the cleaned air back into the atmosphere. I didn't understand the benefits of high humidity until I was introduced to potato storage 25 years later in 2009. Potatoes are dehydrated and shrink if the air is dry. Since dry air shrinks potatoes it is highly profitable to keep them well hydrated.

I built the first very small version of the device I had designed in my head in February, 1985 in Eagle, Idaho and installed it on the stovepipe of a small wood-burning stove. In that test I turned the water black and discharged only a fraction of the smoky particulates from the top of the stove-pipe. It was encouraging but funds were low and I had to make a living, so I moved to eastern Idaho and took a job as a welder and millwright at a sawmill in St. Anthony. The pay was good but it didn't last. They refused to hire me permanently after a physical examination that revealed a deteriorated disk between the lumbar and the sacrum in my lower back. So, I gathered up my wife and two toddler sons and moved to Coeur d' Alene, Idaho where I found work as a welder at a small shop that built sawmill machinery. They didn't require a physical examination and I didn't bring it up. I just worked and endured the lower back pain that was still tolerable at the time.

I met some fine people in Coeur d' Alene, Idaho. One of them was a man that was particularly interested in the concept of air cleaning and emissions control. As we were talking while riding in between Spokane Washington and Post Falls, Idaho one day, he asked me what it would take to get a machine that would do this. I told him that I could get a machine that had been scrapped in Boise that could be modified to perform the process for about $6,000. He said, "*Well, I have $6,000*". That was the beginning of a concentrated effort to prove and commercialize the product for emissions control.

Before the forming of the Environmental Protection Agency there were several states that were addressing the problem of air pollution without federal involvement. In 1955, the U.S. Congress passed the Air Pollution Control Act of 1955. Eight years later came the Clean Air Act of 1963. The Environmental Protection Agency was formed in 1970 by the executive order of Richard Nixon, the Republican President of the United States from 1969 to 1974. The order was ratified by Congress and began to be enforced immediately. In 1990 the Clean Air Act of 1990 was created to address what had become known as "*global warming*" through ozone depletion and to introduce a regulatory policy called Best Available Control Technology (BACT). At it's onset, the EPA the building and headquarters were established in Washington D.C. The building was renamed the William Jefferson Clinton Federal Building in May 2013 after the former president Bill Clinton.

I was concerned about pollution but I was not in favor of putting pressure on industry businesses that they couldn't afford. My attitude was to help businesses to be prepared for the regulation ahead of government interference and to clean themselves up for public relations purposes that would increase public acceptance and good will. After years of taking that approach, I found that that was not going to work. If a particular business' emission was cleaned up, it caused more pressure on every business, including the business that was cleaned because EPA, being an extension of the executive branch of the Federal Government of the U.S., the regulators (the cops) become enamored with the power they have over business and industry. Give a man or a woman a little authority and they will naturally tend toward unrighteous dominion and tyranny. Power corrupts. Such was the case with the EPA and the various state agencies that were set up to comply with the federal law or be penalized by deprivation of federal funds. State agencies became the enforcement arm of the federal government under various names such as the Department of Environmental Quality (DEQ), Commission of Environmental Quality (CEQ), Division of Air Pollution Control DAPC, Air Resources Board (ARB) and others. It was a natural response for industry to resist the regulations wherever they could.

This was going to be a very difficult job, nearly insurmountable for introduction of any new technology to fix an emissions problem. Industrial businesses began to hide what they were doing until caught and avoid being caught by pacification, coverup and deception. I asked a chemist at an oil refinery DMV installation in Nevada if his company was interested in fixing the emission problem or in just pacifying the DEQ. He laughed and responded *"If the DEQ is pacified, we don't have a problem"*. I knew at that point that creating a small business for the purpose of selling emissions control technology in the short term was practically futile. No small business could live with the uncertain schedule that was determined by government control only, and not by the internal motivation of the company that would be targeted as a customer.

Then came Best Available Control Technology, BACT. the new slant on environmental control was encouraging to me. I, in my misunderstanding of the corporate control of clean air technology by crony capitalism, thought that all I had to do was prove that under the new rule my system was the best and I would be in with the EPA and all of the world would have to use my method for emissions control. It was a hard lesson. In retrospect, I expected by practicality to overcome special interests and political connectedness, after all people are basically honest, right? They have to recognize reality and the truth. Wrong! I soon had to face reality for myself. When a new technology is so invasive that it will cause the loss of jobs and political acceptance on a wide scale, truth be damned! Human nature dictates that this is war and all is fair, even if it requires lying and deception to protect your job. Protect the company or you will be left without a position. In other words, compromise your moral principles for money. Money is more important and more necessary than principles or the truth.

The biggest restriction on innovation is resistance. The inventor is treated with ridicule and disdain at first. It has been said that a correct principle endures three reactions before being recognized as truth: First, the purveyor is a crackpot, then he is fiercely opposed until finally he becomes a genius, all of which are false misconceptions. Sheer determination is the most valuable tool in an inventor's constitution. The only thing that separates him from others is the courage to persist and a determination and self-confidence that does not allow him be removed by the naysayers.

After several disappointments I learned that BACT was no savior of new technology. Technology that is invasive to corporations of huge power and political influence is treated as *"dead on arrival"*, mostly because of a factor called NIH (not invented here). If you think you are going to sell your idea to a large company and make a fortune, forget it and develop it on your own. The obstacles are rampant but there are ways if you can keep it afloat. It is like paddling a rowboat through an armada of battleships. Stay the course and hang on when the wakes are high and turbulent.

In 1989 a handful of investors came on board with the exciting new idea of cleaning up atmospheric emissions. As the effort progressed there were several disappointments and failures. Attempts were made to prove different applications and to explore potential markets, some products were tried on sawmill incinerators in Washington and Montana. These trials failed, not because the process didn't work but because wood smoke contains a high resin content and the resin collected disproportionately on the impellers of the test machines and threw them out of balance. I found myself replacing impellers as often as after only four hours of operation, obviously cost prohibitive. I knew the basic scrubber worked but I had to find a different application.

DOES IT REALLY WORK

All truth passes through three stages:
First, it is ridiculed;
Second, it is violently opposed; and Third, it is accepted as self-evident.

-- *Arthur Schopenhauer (1788-1860)*

In 1990 there came an engineer from a French company called Rhone Poulenc. Rhone Poulenc had bought a Stauffer Chemical plant in Silver Bow, Montana that mined and refined elemental phosphorous. Elemental phosphorus is used to make food-grade phosphoric acid, an additive widely used in many products such as matches, soft drinks and several other food products as well as plastics and even toothpaste. The ore they used at the Silver Bow plant contained undesirable substances that were harmful to the environment. These substances were being emitted into the atmosphere as a residue from the kilns used in the process. Among these harmful gases and particulates were a high number of radio active polonium 210 particles that went airborne from the kilns. A good amount of these emitted particles were very small, sub-micron in size. Additional information revealed that Rhone Poulenc was being sued by the State of Montana for violation of their clean air regulations.

The project engineer heard about the scrubbing process I was working on and came to visit me in Post Falls, Idaho. I explained the process to him and he was quite intrigued. However, he stated that he didn't think he could get me on the plant location. I asked him why and he said "*You look like Mickey Mouse*". A salesman that was working with me at the time asked him "*What if it works?*" and he responded that it was a good question. After his return to the plant and some discussion with his boss, I received an invitation to test the process on the Silver Bow plant. I was last. Monsanto, Seimens and others had been there with semi trailer loads of instrumentation and equipment before I showed up with a machine on a trailer behind my pickup truck with a 24 inch impeller and a capacity of 2,000 cubic feet per minute. Sure enough, I looked to the competition like Mickey Mouse.

The system went through 8 different runs on a slip-stream from their kiln. The company that did the tests was Engineering and Environmental Measurement Corporation (EEMC) in Billings, Montana, now known as Bison Engineering. They set up the tests in the customary way as with the others, using a 0.4 micron filter in the analysis for particulates. They also tested for the capture of sulfur dioxide (SO_2), carbon dioxide (CO_2) and fluoride gases. The results were amazing. Particles, including the radioactive polonium 210 as small as 0.4 micron were captured. The CO_2 emission was reduced by approximately 50% on each of the tests. To say the least, this was very encouraging.

DMV SCRUBBER

POLONIUM 205 RADIO ACTIVE PARTICULATE TEST

RHONE POULENC KILN SITE, Butte, Montana

TEST CONDITIONS (<0.4 micron) Grains per dry standard cubic foot (of air) (GR/DSCF)

TEST #1: 21.471 IN - 0.144 OUT

REDUCTION - 93.33%

TEST #3: 19.411 IN - 0.189 OUT

REDUCTION - 99.04%

TEST #4: 8.183 IN - 0.0150 OUT

REDUCTION - 99.82%

TEST #5: 7.000 IN - 0.014 OUT

REDUCTION - 99.80%

TEST #6: 7.105 IN - 0.012 OUT

REDUCTION - 99.83%

TEST #7: 7.040 IN - 0.014 OUT

REDUCTION - 99.80%

TEST #8: 8.985 IN - 0.006 OUT

REDUCTION - 99.93

AVERAGE REDUCTION RATE - 99.65%

DMV SCRUBBER

SULFUR DIOXIDE (SO2) REDUCTION TEST

RHONE POULENC KILN SITE, Butte, Montana

TEST #2-SO2: 1,087 PPM IN - 27 PPM OUT

REDUCTION - 97.5%

TEST #4-SO2: WITH LIME - 762 PPM IN - 224 PPM OUT

REDUCTION - 70.6%

TEST #6-SO2: 681 PPM IN - 95 PPM OUT

REDUCTION - 86.0%

TEST #8: 720 PPM IN - 48 PPM OUT

REDUCTION - 93.3%

DMV SCRUBBER

FLOURIDE REDUCTION TEST

RHONE POULENC KILN SITE, Butte, Montana

TEST #1: REDUCTION - 98.60%

TEST #3: REDUCTION - 98.20%

TEST #5: REDUCTION - 99.60%

TEST #7: REDUCTION - 99.90%

Now what? I didn't know. It took 6 months to get copies of the data and only then upon repeated requests. After some time, I asked the Rhone Poulenc engineer how we did. He said that my invention had outperformed the others by a wide margin. *"How wide"*, I asked, *"about 30%"* was his reply. Well, OK then, lets get going, right? Wrong again. Instead of fixing the emissions problem, Rhone Poulenc decided to shut the plant down rather than fight with the government over emissions, which they did shortly thereafter.

There was another elemental phosphorous plant in Pocatello, Idaho, owned by FMC Corporation at that time. In fact it was probably the biggest producer of elemental phosphorous in the world. I arranged a meeting with the management of that plant and found at least a pacifying interest but it too was soon shut down. Hooray for EPA, right? Put 'em out of business, that will fix the problem, little consideration for the gross national product and the production it takes to sustain a healthy economy. Just another example of federal government mis-management. We could have fixed it and we were too late. Besides, nobody was paying attention to a mouse.

I soon began to realize that fixing emissions was not the goal of the government. Control and dominion overrode practicality then and still does. Power and crony political favoritism corrupts for sure. The corporate ladder is full of pigeon holes. Getting top management to agree with an underlings ideas or desires is too often met with the solid wall of egos and authority. The lower level managers I was talking to, although they liked the idea, could not get past first base with upper management.

Whether or not an idea works does not matter in the corporate government complex (CGC). It is always that familiar perversion of the golden rule, "*the ones with the money make the rules*". In the natural world, as we know it, rules are not governed by the truth. The rules are set and controlled by money and the power of the CGC. The economies of the world are manipulated entirely on the self-interests of those in power, the elite few and the corporations and governments they control. It is a huge mistake for innovators to expect that companies in an applicable business will buy into a new discovery or an idea that tends to upset or disturb their momentum and their precious present methods.

Companies don't buy ideas, they buy companies, usually companies that threaten their business models. I had a long way to go before I would be identified as such a threat. They buy companies either to exploit them for themselves, or if the idea interferes with their established, present momentum, to shelve them and keep them off of the market and out of their way.

When will the truth become the norm? When will lies no longer continue to manipulate and determine the economy and the living standards of citizens throughout the world? When will clean energy and a clean environment be allowed to be the habit? Not until the CGC fails and its lying for gain, enormous wealth and power is widely recognized, which it inevitably will at some point. Any system based on lies and deception is like swiss cheese, it is full of holes and its foundation is very weak. The bigger it gets, the more pressure is placed on its foundation.

It is impossible to protect an antiquated method from better ways with lies and deception in the long term. The result of this trend will eventually be the disintegration of the employee and customer relationships that have held them together. Why? Because liars and manipulators, or at least those who have supported them, eventually discover that they cannot trust themselves nor each other. Mutual respect, based on manipulation and cronyism cannot expect to achieve mutual trust. Truth will eventually prevail but it sure takes a long time for it to happen in the face of worldly skepticism, pride, ignorance and behemoth corporate control of world industry.

After filing the patent in 2004 I was approached by a sign printer in Branson, Missouri. He had somehow heard about my clean air technology and wanted me to make him a machine that would arrest the odor produced by his wide format printer that he used to print outdoor signs. The ink used for outdoor advertising was called true solvent ink. True solvent was used for outdoor sign printing because the print was brighter for more of what was referred to as "pop" and would last longer than alternative inks a the time. The ink used was intolerably odorous for the workers in the work environment. The printer wanted to know if my scrubber would eliminate the odor that was emitted from the true solvent ink printing process. After investigating the chemical base and determining that it was alcohol, knowing that alcohol is soluble in water, I consented to build him a machine.

The machine was installed in a closet in the corner of the sign layout work area. I ran a flexible suction hose up through the false ceiling and about 30 feet over to the room where the printer was operating. The hose was dropped through the interior of a wall and exited out to a location under the printer. I vented the cleaned air from the machine into the ventilation system duct work that was vented over the work area. When the machine was turned on, the odor was completely gone in the shop and the humidity held at a constant around 50% which was ideal for the paper stored in the shop to be used used for printing.

I had captured the odors into the water as I had hoped. The owner was very pleased of course but later, the welding cracked in the bottom of the separation tank and water from the tank leaked into the motor, shorting it out and stopping the process. I replaced it for him one time at no charge but when it happened a second time, I was broke and could not have it repaired again, he had to fix it on his own. It had been a successful test of the process but the design was faulty. R&D can be expensive. The design of the machine had to be changed and I did not have the money to make that change. More doldrums.

CHAPTER FOUR

THE CORPORATE GOVERNMENT COMPLEX

GET OUT OF THE WAY YOU LITTLE PEST

The world is being run and controlled by a consortium of institutional factions that find their origins in economics and business . So, how did this corporate creation of the military, government academic complex come to be? Although it is dominated by current, modern day elite, super rich and powerful people, their current condition finds its roots anciently by those of the same appetite for money and power. The trend started to be prominent and all encompassing with the Roman Empire and its declaration of Christianity by Constantine, which integrated the interests of the government with the interests, or at least a semblance of such interests, into an amalgamation of opposing views in a form that could be sold to and supported by an ignorant and unassuming public. Nobles began to call themselves Christians simply because it became popular to do so. The support of the peace loving public came about as a compromise of principals to a degree that allowed them to live their lives without constant distraction by controversial issues.

While the separation from mother England and the establishment of the new United States of America were proceeding, Patrick Henry, famous for his outspoken protection of freedom, was an influential and immovable force in support of the separation of church and state. The wisdom in such separation can be recognized by observing how wealth, power and control became the driving force of such an incorporation as has been demonstrated by the integration of the Roman Empire with the Roman Catholic Church. That early integration was the beginning of global control over trends and technologies since its establishment 2,000 years ago. It was made easier to sell control to the public under a Christian standard rather than independently or by government alone. It was a fraud, or at very least, a conflict of interests.

The nobles with their individual wealth became the core management of the Holy Roman Empire, finding its roots as early as 330 AD when the Emperor Constantine was purported by a later proven fraudulent document known as the *"Donation of Constantine"* to have given the right to rule over Italy and the whole western world to pope Silvester I sometime between 314 and 335 AD. There was established a classic combining of church and state. Whatever the Catholic Priests said was considered by an ignorant public to be God's law and divine truth. Whenever and wherever that has happened, an elite group of financially well healed property owners have become the dictators of the policies of the church and the policies of the governments of the world that they control. Those policies have never failed to be established by the special, selfish interests of the nobles, then called landgraves, instead of for the best interests of the masses. In other words, governments became dictated by worldly desires, which are selfish and contrary to true christian principals. Any trends or economic interests could now be manipulated, impaired or prevented by the powerful nobles that were controlling the industries that would be invaded by new ways of doing things. Technology would not be accepted nor its development financed without the approval and support of the elite. The modern day petroleum industry is an obvious example, atomic energy and hot fusion another.

Whenever it became, or seemed necessary for a country to go to war with another country, resources were needed to support their war machine. Resources sufficient to fight a war cost a lot of money. From the 8th century forward, significant amounts of money were only available from the nobles who had it. Banks became interim for financing a country's needs, in between the money source and the country. Mayer Amschel Rothschild, founder of the Rothschild family dynasty of European bankers, apprenticed with Jacob Wolf Oppenheimer. Jacob was the son of Simon Wolf Oppenheimer who was the son of Samuel Oppenheimer, Jewish banker, Imperial Court Diplomat and military supplier for the Holy Roman Empire in the 1600s. Samuel advanced a lot of money to support the Great Turkish War of 1683. Rothschild, a court Jew to the German Landgraves of Hesse-Kassel, began issuing international loans in the early 19th century by borrowing money from the Landgrave and loaning it to countries from his interim position as a banker. Landgrave was the title given to nobles of the Holy Roman Empire. The Rothschild banking dynasty was represented by Mayer's five sons who controlled banks in Frankfort, London, Paris, Vienna and Naples. Nathan Rothschild financed the British side of the Napoleonic wars. After the surrender of Napoleon, seeing the trend, he bought up the British bond market and sold the bonds later for a 40% profit, an enormous amount of money.

Governments inherently become quickly corrupted. As voiced by U.S. Senator, Sam Irvin, *"The (U.S.) Constitution was made to guard the people against the dangers of good intentions. There are men of all ages who mean to govern. They promise to be good masters, but they mean to be masters."* Power is addicting. The natural man is drawn to it an initial introduction, followed by a small subscription or compromise and then, like the first dose of heroin or the first alcoholic drink, it calls for more. First it may be abhorred, then compromised until it is finally embraced and put into action. The opposite of love is not hate, it is power. Any person who seeks to have power over another person is not capable of love. Love has no place in government and corporations. Corporations and governments do not have conscience. There is no consideration for the feelings or emotions that make up the souls of human beings, only rules and laws that are needed to control the masses under terms dictated by the self interested control freaks whom have worked their way into the corporate, government establishment.

Before the light bulb, there was kerosene. Prior to 1870, lantern light was fueled by whale oil and was only affordable by the affluent. When kerosene began to replace whale oil, it became available to the middle class and was more widely in demand. At the beginning of the civil war in the United States, the federal government subsidized the production of kerosene and the price rose from $0.35 per barrel to $13.75 per barrel. John D. Rockefeller took advantage of the change in price and thus began first a partnership with the Clark Brothers and evolving through a buyout of the Clarks interests to the beginning of the Standard Oil Company. About 60% of the petroleum found was made into kerosene while it became the habit of a lot of companies to dump the remaining 40% into the rivers and sludge piles with no regard for the environment.

While the motor car had yet to be developed, Standard Oil was producing more than 300 products from petroleum, including roofing tar, paint, chewing gum and Vaseline petroleum jelly. Rockefeller became a millionaire before 1880. Perhaps, control of the entire world's oil industry by Rockefeller was prevented by the Sherman Anti-trust Act and dozens of suits filed by Theodore Roosevelt. After the breakup of Standard Oil Company, Rockefeller's fortune grew to five times what it was before. He finally gave up his ambition to control all of the world's oil business, realizing how unpopular he was becoming with the public. It became the habit of rich and elite moguls such as Carnegie, Rockefeller, Vanderbilt and Morgan to exercise their agendas's in total secret, away from the eyes of the public, setting the stage for the creation of the Federal Reserve by these super rich manipulators of the U.S. economy in 1914.

The health of the planet and its inhabitants is being severely impaired by the pollution created by fossil fuels and nuclear energy. The corporations that support these industries are steeped in tradition, along with the users of their products. Of course, if it is made available, that is what will be used, so petroleum and hot fusion became the norm for the public, who not being informed of any other alternative, were left with no other choice but to use what was made available to them. Now petroleum reserves are running low. It is getting harder and more expensive to extract it from deep in the earth and under the sea. In time petroleum for fuel will be obsolete or replaced by clean energy from water. When that happens the earth will be a better, cleaner place, people will live longer and happier with less disease.

By 1912, President Woodrow Wilson had demonstrably given in to control by the bankers and elitists whom had contributed to his election campaign. He knew that he would not have been elected were it not for their support and financial manipulation of the democratic campaign process. The bankers had placed enough financial support behind Teddy Roosevelt and the Bull Moose party to divert a sizable portion of votes to Roosevelt and away from Wilson's opponent, William Howard Taft and Wilson was elected by a majority of the votes. The Federal Reserve Act passed congress and was signed into law by Wilson and corporate and banker control of, or at least heavy influence on the policies of the government of the U.S. was well on its way. Now it became important for corporate officials with hidden agendas to get themselves appointed to high positions in the executive branch of the government hierarchy, and so they did. The interests of the American people had become of no importance, or at least secondary to the special interests of the elites and their behemoth corporations.

The election of Woodrow Wilson in 1912 paved the way for the passing of the Federal Reserve Act. Wilson was fully aware of who were contributing to his campaign. He later declared: *"Our great industrial nation is controlled by its system of credit. Therefore all of our activities are in the hands of a small group of men who chill and check true economic freedom. We have come to be one of the worst ruled, completely controlled and dominated governments in the world. No longer a government of the majority but a government of opinion and duress of a small group of dominant men." Woodrow Wilson, 1914*

The oil industry has had its hand in government, along with defense manufacturers of military arms and equipment. President Eisenhower warned the people to beware of what he called the "military government complex", referring to the corporations that were in the business of supplying armaments to the United States and others. The government policies became highly manipulated by insiders such as James Baker, Senior Counselor to The Carlyle Group, the business interests of which were heavily invested in United Defense and other supporting companies that were engaged in the hugely profitable business of supporting wars around the world. James Baker served in several high government positions including Secretary of State and White House Chief of Staff under George H.W. Bush. His interests, obviously influenced by the armaments industries, including atomic energy, created a huge special interest skewing of government policies.

The Baker influence is only one example of corporate government control, there are many others. Such control and influence by corporate special interests has created a barrier for the prevention of new invasive technologies such as water for energy and water scrubbing for clean air. It may not seem to be a barrier for water for clean air until it is considered that the false concept of global warming and the Environmental Protection Agency have created enormous amounts of research revenue for colleges and universities as well many companies elected to either study or regulate industrial emissions control around the world. The allocation of revenue to these institutions and companies has created a great deal of support for the special interests of the elite corporate government complex. Atomic energy has done the same.

The real reason Martin Luther King was assassinated by a government operative was to silence him before he led the planned march on Washington DC to further disclose the doings of the Carlyle Group and others who were manipulating the US Government in support of the Viet Nam War since the war was feeding their pocketbooks so profusely. I don't know how many of the US Presidents have been aware or deliberately involved with the corporate, globalist agenda but it is obvious that they have supported it, perhaps with the exception of Andrew Jackson, Abraham Lincoln and John F. Kennedy. In fact, even Woodrow Wilson, who was instrumental in the passing of the Federal Reserve Act, openly admitted that a handful of men with money and power were pulling the strings on the government. His view, as has been that of many others since, was that there is nothing that can be done about it so we just as well cooperate with them. In other words, "*If you can't lick 'em, join 'em.*" That attitude is plainly a dangerous step toward selling ones soul to the devil.

It is amazing and a curious thing what people, by their nature, will do for money and recognition. Aspiration to obtain the honors of men and money motivates the natural man to a dangerous degree and all too often leads to participation in activities related to the dark side of human enterprise. Henry Kissinger has stated his opinion that power is the ultimate aphrodisiac. Power corrupts mankind by morphing into despotism and unrighteous dominion.

Dr. Martin Luther King was not a natural man. A study of King's life and work, his actions and comments can only lead one to the conclusion, that his motivation was to aspire to the works and designs of a higher power by fearless and selfless service to his fellow man. The record demonstrates that MLK could not be bought by power and/or money. Unfortunately for the constitutionally free people of the United States of America, black, white or indifferent, this fact led to his early demise. It certainly wasn't the racial issue.

Had King been allowed to continue, he was on a track that would have revealed to the world the true motivation and globalist mentality involved in the determinations of a few *"elite"* capitalist money mongers since 1914, whose sinister purpose has been to rule the world and control the activities of all of mankind referred to by George H. W, Bush in his now famous *"New World Order"* speech of June 2006 as a *"the rule of law"*, and referring to liberty and freedom as the*"law of the jungle"*.

In April, 1968, one year after making a powerful speech in protest of the decade long war in Vietnam that continued under the Administration of the then President of the U.S., Lyndon Baines Johnson, Martin Luther King was shot to death in Memphis, Tennessee, U.S.A. by a Memphis policeman. The shooting occurred just prior to King's leading a huge protest march on Washington D.C.

After attending a trial in Memphis in 1999, the result of a $100 civil lawsuit brought by Coretta Scott King, Martin's Widow, against Lloyd Jowers, one of the alleged conspirators to the death of her husband, Jim Douglass made the following comments:

"This historic trial was so ignored by the media that, apart from the courtroom participants, I was the only person who attended it from beginning to end. What I experienced in that courtroom ranged from inspiration at the courage of the Kings, their lawyer-investigator William F. Pepper, and the witnesses, to amazement at the government's carefully interwoven plot to kill Dr. King. The seriousness with which US intelligence agencies planned the murder of Martin Luther King, Jr. speaks eloquently of the threat Kingian nonviolence represented to the powers that be in the spring of 1968. Thirty-two years after Memphis, we know that the government that now honors Dr. King with a national holiday also killed him. As will once again become evident when the Justice Department releases the findings of its 'limited re-investigation' into King's death, the government is continuing its coverup just as it continues to do in the closely related murders of John and Robert Kennedy and Malcolm X."

The checks and balances system, set up by the founders of the United States provided three distinct divisions of the U.S. government, Legislative, Executive and Judicial. Thomas Jefferson warned future generations not to ever let the powers of government become concentrated in the Executive Branch or we would have tyranny. The free people of the United States should be alarmed that the actions of the Executive Branch are simply referred to as actions by the government when it is clearly the autonomous actions of the Executive Branch, and most often without the support of either of the other two branches.

Too bad the mainstream media does not make the distinction clear, but then one must consider who owns the mainstream media. Another problem with seeking truth through the media is that the nature of the common man leans to consider anyone who is on television to be honest, informed and smart. It is becoming increasingly more evident that all too often this is not the case so much as that the *"talking heads"* aspire to the honors of men and money more than to the honors of truth. After all, they would not be on television without the support of the owners of the networks, so they rationalize that a little truth is better than none at all and thereby justify their positions. The real problem is not that they don't tell the truth, it is that they don't tell the whole truth, when it is the whole truth that holds the key to preservation of freedom. Half truths are worthless, misleading and dangerous.

Martin Luther King's speech against the war in Vietnam included the following comments:

"A true revolution of values will soon look uneasily on the glaring contrast of poverty and wealth. With righteous indignation, it will look across the seas and see individual capitalists of the West investing huge sums of money in Asia, Africa, and South America, only to take the profits out with no concern for the social betterment of the countries, and say, 'This is not just.' It will look at our alliance with the landed gentry of South America and say, 'This is not just.' The Western arrogance of feeling that it has everything to teach others and nothing to learn from them is not just."

What do you think? Did this speech bring the corporate establishment to implement the elimination of a powerful influence against their clandestine plan to rule?

Sam Ervin, special counsel and chairman of the Committee on Government Operations during the investigation of the Nixon Administration, 1974 (watergate) said this: *"The Constitution was made to guard the people against the dangers of good intentions. There are men of all ages who mean to govern. They promise to be good masters, but they mean to be masters. The Constitution was written primarily to keep the Government from being masters of the American people."* Sam Ervin

Sam Ervin was a Democrat. Do you think it matters one way or the other what political party he espoused? The real problems arise and fall with the determinations of each individual, not the political parties that they support. There are those with good intentions and bad intentions in both parties. As long as the global elitists can keep the people of a country focused on the under issues and arguing amongst themselves on a political level, whether on the street or on radio or television, it keeps their focus off of the whole truth and off of them until they can complete their clandestine and sinister agenda. Keep an eye out and you will see that their confidence has now grown to the point that they are sure of themselves, that they will definitely prevail and are now making it more public.

There are those, and the numbers are growing rapidly, that would support a freedom protection plan. This has been profoundly demonstrated by the recent rush and demand for firearms and ammunition by the citizens of the United States in response to a move by the Executive Branch to take more control of the firepower demanded by the second amendment of the U.S. Constitution. Will this eventually lead to an old western type showdown? Will the policemen of the Executive Branch enforcement arm of government support the Executive Branch to take over as has been done by such force on other occasions in the history of the world? They were good soldiers that crucified Christ.

If you think that conspiracy is only a theory, you are right where the conspirators want you to be. Conspiracies have been around ever since the creation of mankind and also the creation of a company. Company leaders have conspired from their outset to develop a successful business model. These designs are kept secret in order to have an advantage over their competition. Company conspiracies have evolved into conspiracies in government by the development of the corporate government establishment. Wherever the globalist's imperial system has been implemented in the world, the result has been an increase in poverty and starvation for the countries that have become indebted to it. The United States is rapidly on the verge of following suit. Poverty is looming as a desire for worldwide parity is pushed by the corporate elitists and if it happens it is all brought about by conspiracies.

Now, let it be known that this writer respects the rights to make choices by individuals, whatever those choices might be. However, it is imperative that before a stand can be taken, and the responsibility that comes with that stand, one must have all of the information necessary to take it with conviction. Another choice is to have no conviction, to remain asleep and do nothing, trusting that others will make the right stand on your behalf. If that is your choice, you are already on the side of the those who would have you subservient to all of their self aggrandizing whims. History is clear, the crucifixion of Christ was supported by ignorant people with no individual conviction. These are those by whom issues are ignored and who would have a king to be responsible for their actions and choices, they are the *"king makers"*. Where do you stand? Can you be bought or are you a subscriber of what Patrick Henry so eloquently put forth in a powerful speech urging the Continental Congress to sign the Declaration of Independence? *"Is life so dear or peace so sweet as to be purchased at the price of chains and slavery?"*

Information disclosed by the New York Times in 2014 about J. Edgar Hoover and the FBI's determination to censor Martin Luther King prompted me to write further about King and his relationship with a U.S. Government, a government aligned with a globalist agenda to protect and defend not the citizens of the United States but the Government <u>from</u> the citizens. A recent issue of the New York Times has disclosed a letter that was written by an FBI Agent, assigned by his Director, J. Edgar Hoover as an apparent attempt to persuade King to commit suicide. The letter was delivered to King prior to his journey to Norway to accept the Nobel Peace Prize but was not opened until after his return. King, having had previous experiences with the FBI, immediately suspected that the letter had originated with them. It has since been confirmed that indeed that was the case.

It is interesting to note that J. Edgar Hoover, a known bachelor, cross dresser and homosexual, associated with and blackmailed by the Mafia used sexual misbehavior as a tool to discredit King. It was apparently the best that could be found against the civil rights leader. I guess people in power at some point begin to believe they are exalted, that they are invincible, untouchable and exempt from the moral standard widely accepted by the citizens they have been appointed to serve. Transfer and accusation of bad behavior to an opposing party is commonly practiced and easy to rationalize because persons who believe and behave a certain way naturally assume that others will see things and act or react in the same ways they do.

Which one was the real evil one when the finger was pointed by J. Edgar Hoover toward Martin Luther King? How much more of this kind of evil is residual today with a White House whose operations have been so obviously dictated by the globalist agenda? Nothing has changed in this respect. That fact, has been, and is becoming more obvious the same today as it was with Hoover.

Martin Luther King, , Coretta's attorney, William Pepper and others had the courage to make a choice. Standing firmly with Patrick Henry they pledged their lives, their fortunes and their sacred honor just as the founders did when this great, free country was established. Was it for the honors of men or for money? Obviously not. Who among us has that kind of courage? It is impossible to support both sides of the issue because it is impossible to serve two masters at the same time, but these courageous people chose to defend to their death the right to freely make these important choices. Has the time come when we will be forced to take a stand for one side or the other?

The disclosures made by whistle blower, Edward Snowden were not the only evidences uncovered by other patriots on these issues. The corporations, Bechtel, The Carlyle Group, Halliburton, J.P. Morgan Chase, World Bank, International Monetary Fund and their operative organization called the Federal Reserve and several others have had fingers and representatives in the U.S. Government, particularly the Executive Branch, at least since the enactment of the Federal Reserve Act in 1914. Their influence becomes more evident and more widespread, rapidly since the financial meltdown of 2008. Scandals of criminal and civil disobedience, although rampant and plainly evident among Wall Street Bankers, have been protected by this corrupt and greedy corporate/government establishment by dictating that the US Justice Department Attorney General under Obama, Eric Holder ordered the Department of Justice to back off of from pursuing fraud charges against the criminals in the banking system.

The corporate/government establishment has used the United States CIA, a bureau administered by the Executive Branch to accomplish its imperialistic takeover of third world countries on many occasions since its creation in 1947. Such imperialism began with the creation of the CIA, the overthrow of the democratic government of Iran in 1953 and then the takeover of Guatemala in 1954, instigated by the Dulles Brothers and the CIA for United Fruit Company. The United Fruit propaganda was an early experiment to use communism as a tool to capture public support for their actions. The then democratically elected President of Guatemala, Jacobo Arbenz, because he was trying to take back the land for the Guatemalan people that had been arbitrarily granted (for a large sum of money of course) to United Fruit Company by the previous dictator, Jorge

Ubico, was branded as a communist and the word circulated through the media to the people in the United States to gain support for a takeover. Arbenz was ousted and a military dictator, Carlos Castillo Armas, was arbitrarily installed in his place. PLEASE don't try to convince me anymore that the United States Government and the CIA support democracy. The evidence is too clear that the opposite has nearly always been the case.

A most interesting experiment in US imperialism was the ousting of democratically elected President of Iran, Mohammad Mosaddegh, and his replacement with a lackey dictator, the Shah of Iran in order to preserve the oil interests of both Britain and the United States from the Iranian people. The experiment, spearheaded by Kermit Roosevelt, a CIA operative worked quite well. Hence, it has been used to implement imperialism on many occasions since and is still being used on a larger scale today in the middle east. The system is simple; stir up insurrections beginning with paid mercenaries and escalating to larger groups of militants such as Jihadists to ISIS, then step in as the saving hero by taking over the country and its resources, all at the expense of the US taxpayers and others. ISIS and Islamic Jihad rebels became a scaled up version of the same tactics learned and exercised in Iran in 1953 and in Guatemala the following year.

Because of the unscrupulous business practices of a few huge banks and corporations that are owned and controlled by an elite few, the economy of the U.S. is now on the brink of collapse. Inflation looms as a threat to the paychecks of all workers and the modest to moderate incomes of small businesses. Because interest rates are already at zero, the only tool left for the Federal Reserve Bank is to print more money to keep up with the national debt. Printing more money makes trading partners like Europe and China angry and devalues the dollar for all American citizens. Interest rates will rise and commodity prices will rise rapidly, they have to now. There is no other choice.

It is hard to make a stand when your welfare depends on compliance with a system that can take everything you have. Creating poverty and keeping people poor has its advantages for the elite few. A weak people, the king makers, poses no threat to the rich and powerful, that is until the proverbial mouse is backed into a corner and is finally left with no other choice. Then he will probably bite somebody.

It is time for all good Americans, whether or not they work for the private sector, the government, law enforcement, military, muslim, jew, christian, black, white or whatever to wake up and establish a position and become proactive in support of a position, whether for or against the globalist enslavement plan and agenda. Such a position is essential for personal growth and progress. The king makers have no place in the Pollyanna Zone.

In compliance with the tax and spend solution offered by Keynesian economics which was adopted by Franklin D. Roosevelt as the solution to fix poverty in the United States in 1933, rocket science, atomic energy and global warming came to be more attractive endeavors, not because they were the right or most practical solutions to air pollution or aeronautical and space development but rather because they were the most expensive. The more expensive the program, the more control required because these enormous endeavors could not possibly be handles with the limited resources of small business, or not even by that of substantial companies without government support.

The government, its corporate backers and the bankers that supported the corporations that controlled the executive branch were placed fully in control of programs. The powerful, elite bankers and corporate individuals whose influences practically control the government, were protected, packaged and sold by them to the masses to be important and necessary. Clean air and clean energy, being simple, cheap and easy to do, were out advertised and not supported. They did not stand a chance.

CHAPTER FIVE

DOWN BUT NOT OUT

WHY KEEP BANGING YOUR HEAD ON A WALL WHEN ALL IT DOES IS MAKE YOUR HEAD SORE

While pursuing these efforts to succeed with what genuinely appeared to be an opportunity to turn the technology into a profitable business, there were a few investors who had taken confidence in what I was trying to do because they thought that the venture could be enormously profitable. Among them was a man that was a senior manager at a large securities firm on Wall Street in New York City. His job at the firm was in corporate mergers and acquisitions. He heard about my small company from someone and came to Post Falls to investigate. After some due diligence on his part, he committed to invest $90,000 in the venture and made a good faith payment toward his commitment by buying shares of the company stock. I later realized that it was his intention to take over the company. After all, his expertise included hostile takeover methods that he had learned and the had been exemplified by Boone Pickens in the Texas oil industry.

After seeking out the company debts and assets, which were few and insignificant, he came to the little shack I had moved my family to in Mullan, Idaho after losing our home in Coeur d' Alene.

The floors were warped in the Mullan house and the foundation was crumbling so the couch that he sat down on to address me was a little slanted. He stated that the little house reminded him of the house that his parents had and I wondered how much charity he felt for his parents. He quickly stated his mission. He had come to talk me into bankrupting the company. Although he didn't say so, I surmised that his intention was to acquire the assets, including the technology. However, he had evidently overlooked the fact that there was no technology to be had other than what was in my head at the time since we had never gotten out of research and development mode and a patent had yet to be applied for. It became clear to me that he did not care about the other investors either. I still clung to the hope of finding a way to succeed on their behalf and mine. John Peterson had told him that if he messed with me he would wind up with the biggest empty sack he had ever seen. However, I later included him with the other investors in a royalty contract I later established with a Pennsylvania company.

Having failed in developing a way to scrub sawmill incinerator emissions without caking the impellers and the discouraging experience of attempting to solve problems for companies that elected to shut down rather than subject themselves to the costs of government intervention, I could not find a way to proceed with the effort. I had to find another way to make a living for my family. I could no longer justify to myself the acquisition of capital from small investors to only hit the wall of disappointment with no returns for them on their investments. My wife had gotten a job at a car dealer in Kellogg, Idaho and was paying the rent and groceries. A fresh herb distribution business I had established to sustain us was taken away from me by the supplier in San Diego. By 1992 I was broke again and left with no job nor any way to earn in Mullan, Idaho.

Some time after losing everything of material I had, I was able to buy an old, discarded police car from a dealer in Kellogg. The car had a blown head gasket but a mechanic in the area showed me how to temporarily plug the leak in the gasket by adding house pepper to the radiator fluid. It worked and would keep the gasket from leaking water into the oil for short periods and the white smoke out the tail pipe would subsist for a few hundred miles. I drove the car to Pocatello where I had attended college before and, with the help of a student loan, I registered for a semester at Idaho State University and re-entered academia. I was attracted to ISU because of their new environmental engineering department. I soon became acquainted with Solomon Leung, a professor in that department and after our introduction, I wrote and presented to him the following white paper entitled:

"Hydropermutation and Comparative Technologies Discussion."

The hydropermutation process is a chemical process reducing cold water droplets into sub-micron sizes and introducing hot flue gases simultaneously into a violent, frictional and turbulent atmosphere wherein battering of the droplets and gases together creates a frictional, kinetic environment wherein certain chemical and ionic changes are more apt to occur, including but not limited to kinematic eddy viscosity alterations, free movement particle transport affects or Brownian motion, solvation, solvolysis, hydrolysis and solution. This environment is produced by using an atomizer impeller or other paddle wheel device to produce droplets as small as 10 micron and splattering these tiny droplets on an anvil or against a wall at close proximity and at a speed of 15,000 to 24,000 feet per minute to accomplish further size reduction to sub-micron size range; to place an inertial and kinetic stress on the gas particles and to control and force the collisions of the reduced droplets with particulate matter or gas particles for more efficient control and collection of the gas and particulates into solution.

In order to provide a better understanding of the process, the following facts are provided:

1. When a 3,000 micron drop of water falls from a height of 18 inches onto a hard surface it breaks into ten (10) pieces.

2. If the height of release of the water drop is increased the same drop breaks into more pieces because of an increased force of impact on contact with the hard surface,

Using these known facts as foundation it follows that the accelerated impacting of pre-atomized 10 micron droplets decreases their size to sub-micron range. Controlled multiple collisions of these fine droplets with particulates and sub-micron size gas particles in low pressure zones causes a more efficient chemical change and mixing of gas with liquid because of exponentially increased opportunities for droplet surface to particle contact, adsorption and absorption.

The formation of clouds in the atmosphere has proven in acid rain studies to be an affective means for the collection of sulfur dioxide, nitrogen oxides and other particles. The gas molecules and particulates provide collection points for the formation of water droplets. When these droplets become sufficient size they fall to the earth as rain, carrying with them the various concoctions produced by chemical reactions occurring during their formation. Among these concoctions, of course, are acids and other pollutants which cause unfavorable affects on the environment.

Possibly the most significant basis for the scrubbing efficiency of clouds is the small droplet size and their uniformity and colloidal dispersion. This natural process precludes the problem of droplet interfacial tension which ordinarily disallows the intrusion of particles into the droplets interior after the droplet has been formed. Since clouds are such efficient collectors of gases and particulates, it seems reasonable to assume that devices designed to collect gases and particulates from flue gas emissions could obtain maximum efficiency with the employment of smaller and smaller droplets.

The development of wet scrubber technology has attained a practical limit at 40 microns droplet water nozzle applications for three reasons:

1. The energy requirement to further reduce droplet sizes is costly.

2. Efficient means of particle/droplet contacting has not been satisfactorily established.

3. Mist collection of super fine, low pH droplets has been difficult because of droplet re-entrainment problems.

A type of mechanical dust collector originated with the injection of water into the intake of a standard blower with a limited amount of success. Standard blowers have been designed to accomplish the smooth transfer of air without turbulence. Pumps are designed in the same manner and with the same end in mind, that is the smooth, efficient transfer of fluid with the least amount of resistance. The application of such a design for scrubbing will produce at best, an accidental surface contact or collision of particles with droplets since the particles and droplets are traveling smoothly by purpose of the design along the same paths and in the same direction with one another and through wider and wider passages through the blower chamber. This type of scrubber, although having a degree of effectiveness for dust collection has proven inefficient for the collection of sub-micron particles and gases and therefore has no significant application in emissions control.

A wet system that is commonly used is the venturi scrubber. The venturi scrubber was originated with the idea of squeezing the fluid and particles together through a narrow neck as opposed to the wider affect of the fan, to create an increased velocity and decreased pressure in order to reduce surface tension interference in the mixing process. The venturi method provides somewhat improved particle/droplet contacting than the standard wet scrubber for mist collection. The contacting is done however with the same application and affect as the original fan dust collector in that the particles and droplets are all traveling in the same direction, parallel with one another.

U.S. patent #4,469,498 discloses more efficient means for the enhancement of a venturi scrubber. Mist particles become more readily collected in unidirectional flow because of compatibility with additional fluid. Accelerating the fluid of a venturi scrubber decreases pressure and surface tension in the fluid which promotes the effect of water/particle adsorption. A method was introduced for enhancing the collection of a venturi type system by varying the closure of the throat in the atomizer accompanying a venturi process. This causes an increase in the pressure drop and an enhancement of collection effectiveness of the venturi scrubber. The collection efficiency of a venturi scrubber severely drops off for the collection of particles smaller than 1 micron in size. Even when using a high pressure drop of as much as 40 inches, less than 80% collection efficiency is observed below 0.5 micron as demonstrated with the John Zink venturi scrubber, used in one application in an attempt to arrest 0.4 micron radio nuclide particles. Major limiting factors in the use of venturi systems are high energy costs to achieve efficiencies in the sub-micron range, the large volumes of scrubbing fluid required and the accompanying containment and disposal problems.

Standard wet scrubbers are most often used for dust and airborne particle collection. Standard wet scrubbers use either a water bath through which to pass the gases or they may employ some type of droplet particle contacting means within a tank. Water bath systems are greatly ineffective since the gas bubbles containing particles and gases largely pass through the bath without contacting the particles with the water. The problem of discharging particles into the atmosphere is also experienced with wet scrubbers since sufficient drop in temperature is not accomplished to condense the droplets into solution and they are lost in the discharged gas stream.

In the droplet spray application, the droplets are introduced from a spray nozzle or nozzles, at a size of about 40 microns at the top of the scrubber tank and the gases are introduced into the bottom of the tank. The droplets and particles are expected to collide within the medium and be absorbed into the solution. Collisions occurring in this environment have proven to be inefficient because of the natural dodging action of the particles and droplets from one another. This process also shows insufficient temperature drop for condensing and re-entrainment of solution.

Standard wet scrubbers show limited efficiency for sulfur dioxide reduction and little affect in the reduction of sub-micron particle emissions. One reason for the limited collection affect of standard wet scrubber systems is the interfacial tension of large droplets. The collection of particles is limited and dependent upon contacting on the surfaces of the droplets. There is also the problem of back mixing. Back mixing is caused by the less than perfect distribution of droplets and large droplets falling faster than small ones and the spray also being applied to the walls of the scrubber chamber and baffles. The deposition of the fluid to the walls and baffles of the system wastes the effect of a large percentage of the scrubbing fluid. Back mixing renders a good deal of the scrubbing fluid useless for collection due to interfacial tension of droplets and surface tension of the water curtains formed on the walls.

The use of pneumatics has been unattractive for most scrubbing applications because the high pressure drop required to accomplish the processes results in unacceptably high energy costs. These costs are compounded by the necessity of industry to treat high volumes of gases, thereby making the treatment of a necessary flue gas stream cost prohibitive.

Rotary atomization of fluid droplets will reduce their size to about 10 microns. It is significant to note that rotary atomization can be made to produce more consistent sized droplets. The speed of the atomizer will regulate the size of the droplets. The configuration of the atomizer disk will regulate the consistency. The rotary atomizer has demonstrated that it is the most affective and efficient method known for droplet size reduction and size control.

The transfer function of the medium in a hydropermutation system has the affect of a venturi system in that it decreases pressure by increasing velocity of a combination of the gas/water stream which principal is applied with a venturi scrubber. A decreased pressure of the gas/water stream in the hydropermutation system allows for more ready adherence of the gas particles with the water droplets. Rotary atomization of cold water droplets applied simultaneously with the acceleration and impaction of the hot flue gas stream, causes thermal enhancement of collection efficiencies, splattering of the droplets and gases and the tangential zig zag flow of the droplets and gases through a restricted zone to create frictional, kinematic and more effective particle/droplet contacting means for chemical reactions to occur and for the more efficient mixing of particles and gases into solution. This constitutes the main embodiments of a hydropermutation process.

Hydropermutation process systems induce their own draft and can be scaled up or down to retrofit individually or in series to existing flues for a quick fix to industrial emissions problems. The retrofit approach to scrubbing upgrade is a definite benefit to small industrial businesses since the upgrade costs are low, the retrofits can be systematically phased in and they can be made without absorbing the profits of the company.

The hydropermutation process is applied by simple atomization and collision technologies in concert with one another and the results of their combined applications are surprisingly affective. The process reduces the fluid droplets by atomization and splattering to as small size as possible. Flue gas is treated in the same gas stream and application to accomplish a forced collision of the gas particles with the liquid droplets, prohibiting the ordinary dodging action and premature back mixing as is experienced with ordinary wet scrubber methods. When fluid and gases travel simultaneously with one another in a tangential flow, splattering back and forth from impeller to target plate, the constant rebounding of particles with droplets causes countless collisions to occur. Because of the tangential flow of the mix, the forced collisions of the hydropermutation process occur many times prior to exiting a hydropermutation chamber. Forced contacting of the sub-micron sized droplets wit6h the sub-micron size particles creates an efficient reorganization of soluble particles into solution. The collection gases such as NOx which has less solubility, can also be enhanced because of the increased opportunity for contacting to occur. Crowding the medium with surface instead of volume allows for more absorption to occur.

A calculation of the surfaces of scrubbing fluid droplets can be accomplished by a simple calculation of spherical volumes. If a 40 micron droplet is reduced to 20 micron droplets, just half the size, 8 droplets are created. To reduce the same 40 micron droplet to droplets 25% the size or 10 micron, will create 64 droplets. Most importantly, the surface area of the liquid is increased exponentially as well, creating 16 times the water surface to be exposed to particle collection by simply reducing a droplet size. Splattering will further enhance the surface exposure of the liquid. This affect causes the hydropermutation process to obtain an increase in droplet to particle exposure occurrence by as much as 25,000 times more than the standard wet scrubber systems. that use 40 micron droplet sprays.

NOx particles are notoriously difficult to trap in solution since the particles may be taken up in one of 10,000 contacts with a solution. Hydropermutation increases the number of opportunities for contacting to occur and to force their occurrence. It follows empirically that the absorption of NOx particles will be increased as a result of this enhanced interaction. Since gases such as SO2, chlorine, etc. are water soluble, more efficient contacting of gas/liquid is enough to enhance the collection effectiveness of hydropermutation over standard wet scrubber methods.

Since hydropermutation requires the use of a high pressure fan, the replacement of induced draft fans in boiler systems becomes reasonable. The use of an intake damper to control the burn and enough hydropermutation fan capacity to transfer the required amount of air will accomplish the scrubbing process and will result in the elimination of the need for an induced draft fan and its horsepower requirement. The economics of a hydropermutation application replaces some of the processes of a standard system such as transfer fans, bag houses or electrostatic precipitators. The actual costs of installation and operation of such devices can be offset very quickly.

Hydropermutation equipment is modular and is designed with quick change wear parts for accommodating abrasion intensive wood hog fuels and the abrasive mineral contents of coal ash. Wear parts can be changed in each individual hydropermutation unit within 20 minutes without interruption of plant operations. Continuous blowdown of large particulate matter provided no dead spots in the system for accumulation of residue. Down time for scrubber maintenance is totally eliminated with a hydropermutation system. Since the system handles both large and small particulates simultaneously there is no need for bag-house or multi-cone support. Ash disposal is handled by a sludge pump at the bottom of a liquid/solid separation tank. Waste water is recycled by the system so there is no significant water discharge into the environment. Comprehensive, enclosed handling of both air and water provides maximum environmental compliance at a reasonable cost.

Further research points toward the possibility for NOx reduction by this process because of the turbulent hammering of the gases in a hydropermutation chamber. There have been several, mostly unsuccessful attempts to enhance the solubility of NOx by converting NO to NO2. There is a wide diversity of opinions regarding the solubility of NOx. Based on current knowledge it is probably valid to conclude that NOx is soluble only under certain conditions. The demonstration of these conditions will require additional experience and research.

Confidence for significant reduction of NOx by hydropermutation is maintained in spite of the fact that some experts believe that there is no more development or improvement to be done in wet scrubbing technology. This confidence is based upon experience with solid particle reduction and liquid droplet size reduction and mixing. Further tests of the hydropermutation process will show if it is possible to mechanically break the valence of the nitrogen/oxygen particles by stress and turbulent contacting in a sub-micron environment. Further collection may be caused by the forced collisions of sub-micron water droplets with the nitrogen/oxygen combinations. It is logical to assume that the collection efficiency of the hydropermutation system over 40 micron droplet spray manifold systems will be enhanced by tens of thousands of times since surface exposure of the droplets is increased by such a rate.

The hydropermutation process visual opacity tests have successfully demonstrated the arrest of nearly 100% of 0.4 micron P205 particles from the smoke stream created by burning elemental phosphorous. Wood waste demonstrations and tests produced a permanently retained opacity of the liquid effluent derived from the hydropermutation process. These experiments with opacity and effluent tests show excellent results. A conclusion must be drawn that with a hydropermutation process application sub-micron particle collection efficiency is achieved at its greatest possible potential by this method when using water alone as a collection means.

Additional scientific theory suggests that some additional phenomenon may occur in the sub-micron droplet/particle environment created by hydropermutation. Brownian motion has been observed below 0.5 micron. When the water droplets are being reduced to such a size, then it would be of benefit toward the reintegration of the contents into the scrubbing liquor. The reduction of droplets to sub 0.5 micron size in an efficient manner by mechanical means and the reconstruction of the droplets in the mist collector, integrated with any respective community of gas molecules causes an accumulation of all soluble ingredients into solution.

Regardless of these considerations, it must be concluded that, as far as wet scrubbing is concerned, hydropermutation offers the most affective technology available for the collection of both large and sub-micron particles together in the same process. It is also suggested that if it is possible to significantly reduce NOx using only wet scrubbing without additive support, hydropermutation has the best chance of doing so. At any rate, particles smaller than 10 microns which may cause the opacity of a flue gas stream, are proven to be significantly and economically reduced by a hydropermutation process. Installation and operating costs are lower and collection efficiencies higher than with any other system known to date.

Looking back in retrospect, I didn't have a practical comprehension of what I was talking about. I was struggling to understand the technology better and to get attention enough to find the confidence and capital necessary to proceed with the effort. I had too much information not to have confidence that I was on to something very important. Few people had the patience to read all of that but there was one at Idaho State University Environmental Engineering Department, Dr. Solomon Leung. He read it and was impressed enough to condense it into a page and a half abstract that he presented at a clean air symposium in Atlanta, Georgia. His presentation led to licensing of the technology to Selas Fluid Processing, a company in Pennsylvania that manufactured hazardous waste incinerators.

Selas Fluid Processing and T-Thermal were subsidiaries of Linde AG, a very large German corporation. The contract I signed with them provided a 4% royalty to be shared by myself and the investors whom had contributed to the R&D effort. My confidence was high but my hands were tied by them for 11 years by a confidential disclosure agreement. After the expiration of our 11 year contract, I called the new President of the company, the third one since the outset of the effort, and asked him what he wanted to do with the technology. He showed little interest in pursuing the effort after what he said to be a $600,000 investment by the company in research and development. He said they had built a 10,000 cfm unit. The impeller was scaled up from the prototype I had sent them. The scaled up version of the device was set it up on a chemical plant in New Jersey. The testing ran for 6 months and showed promise but they had not decided to go forward with it. Peter Falcone, the project engineer that managed the R&D on the system for Selas wrote an impressive white paper when working on the project. His comments in developing and evaluating the data were very favorable and I was again encouraged that the system could soon go to market. He recorded the following comments on what he had found during his preliminary tests.

"Data from this first test was very promising which prompted the conduct of an extended test run which would yield data from a wide variety of waste feed compositions. .... Side by side comparison of the HYDROP (their name for the DMV device) *technology to other venturi scrubbers and a wet electrostatic precipitator provide its viability in this application considering the implications of MACT* (EPA acronym for maximum achievable control technology) *and other regulatory restrictions. Continued development work, including scale up plans is highlighted..... The HYDROP scrubber removed 84 to 94% of the particulate matter contained in the slipstream treated. The output of the HYDROP was consistently below the 0.03 gr/dscf particulate emission limit proposed by the MACT standards."*

The heavy metal particulates that were removed by the HYDROP scrubber in the Selas preliminary tests were antimony, arsenic, silver, barium, cadmium, chromium, lead and mercury, mercury being removed at the rate of 93%. Needless to say I was encouraged and hopeful that the project would continue and the device would soon proceed to market. It never happened. It never got out of R&D.

Years passed. I started a finance company and pursued other means of income while I tried to figure out why Selas did not go forward with the technology. Nobody in the company was telling me why not. I finally had to figure it out for myself, as I learned how the EPA and the state air quality agencies worked. Selas's customers were getting new air quality permits by simply making improvements to their burning processes. The obvious question for them at that point was why would Selas want to cure the problem at the tail pipe when improvements to the incinerators they were selling would satisfy the EPA or state agency air quality permits for their customers. If they were to come up with a high performance scrubber, they would shoot themselves in the foot with their core business. Small improvements to their incinerators would sell new models and more incinerators. Duh….. economically, it was a nobrainer.

Sawmill incinerators had been much the same, however, I think they were more inclined to solve their emissions problem at the tail pipe and be done with it because they were smaller businesses and made quicker decisions. Putting aside government controls and regulations would, in their view, let them get on with their business models without further restriction. They were in the lumber business, not the selling of incinerators, Too bad that wood smoke contained so much resin, acting like glue and caking the impellers of the DMV and throwing them out of balance in short order.

There were other incineration facilities that I looked into including medical waste and garbage. According to Energy Recovery Council figures in 2011, waste to energy plants in communities across the United States produced about 2,700 megawatts of energy, enough to power 2 million homes. It is a good idea but their emissions from these incinerators introduce a myriad of particulates and chemicals to the atmosphere because of the diverse types of materials being incinerated. This problem has created a need for better emissions control. I saw this as a possible opportunity to introduce DMV to the waste to energy industry.

I became aware of a new municipal waste to energy plant that had been built in Spokane Washington not too far from my shop in Post Falls, Idaho. I arranged for a tour of the plant and learned a lot there. The incineration temperature for waste to energy plants is up to 2,000°F in order to burn the menagerie of materials found in municipal waste. The metals are removed in these processes by magnets before the remainder is moved on to the incinerator but a variety of heavy metals are left in the household waste after the removal of the magnetic material?

I could see that the emissions control used for this application consisted of more than one step. A baghouse (huge vacuum bag) was used for the capture of large particulates, carbon injections to absorb heavy metals, dioxins and furans and a wet scrubber at the end that used the injection of lime to raise the pH and reduce the emission of acid gases. A method that had been developed by Exxon was used that introduced ammonia into the burner to react with the nitrogen to reduce the emission of NOX. Probably one of the biggest benefits of waste to energy incinerators is the burning of methane that is generated from garbage in landfills and emitted to the atmosphere at random.

There are two important problems with burning any kind of materials at temperatures in excess of about 1,600°F. One is the rapid production of oxidized nitrogen (NOX) that results in photochemical smog in the atmosphere and the other is the acceleration in the production of poisonous gases (dioxins). Incinerators such as fluidized bed systems have been used to lower the burn temperature below the production threshold of these materials with good success in reducing the emissions but they cannot eliminate them entirely. However, such an improvement has been found to qualify some companies for a new air quality permit, buying more time and kicking the can down the road for a little longer with the air quality bureaucrats while they concentrate on their core business models that produce the revenue to keep them competitive and profitable. The decisions in any company are almost always made by choosing the least costly or the most profitable option. If the length of time allocated in an air quality permit is long enough to offset the cost of the changes contemplated to the system needed to comply with a regulation, it is opted to select that path to satisfy a compliance requirement.

During the development of the DMV, I was exposed to two major coal fired power plants. I met in Salt Lake City with an environmental engineer that was with Utah Power and Light, a public utility that supplied electricity to a large grid covering Utah and Idaho. The UP&L grid was part an integral part of a power loop that circled the entire western states from California to Washington on the coast and down through Montana, Idaho, Utah and Arizona. Each utility in the network would share power, alternating demand during peak times for some areas while demand was lower in others. This cooperative sharing system lent itself to more convenient distribution but it also increased vulnerability in the event of a potential major power failure caused by a natural disaster or deliberate sabotage.

Companies providing power to and sharing power with this western power loop were numerous. Some directly owned by the public called public utility companies and some were private utilities that tied into the grid for a contracted price. Electricity is generated mostly by coal in Utah and Arizona, and by hydro-electric power in Idaho, Washington and Oregon. Power dams along the Columbia River provided a great deal of the power for the loop and particularly for the northwest. I was of course interested in helping the coal fired plants to overcome rapidly growing regulations that put more and more pressure on environmental emissions.

Although nuclear power plants had grown to a large number by this time, coal fired power plants and their burning of coal to generate electricity produced the majority of the power being generated in the United States. I thought this fact would open doors for the DMV to be applied to satisfy the emissions problems of coal fired power plants. I had the attention of the environmental engineer in charge of UP&L emissions and compliance requirements. He liked the idea. Together we made a trip to Kemmerer, Wyoming where UP&L had a 700 megawatt coal fired power plant in operation at the time. Our objective was to establish a slip stream from one of their stacks to determine and prove the effectiveness of the DMV for intercepting the harmful particulates and gases from the emitted gas stream.

A lot of uncertainty existed at the time because it was not clear what political pressure against the use of coal would prevail at the federal level. There was a lot of discussion about alternative solutions to the emissions problems of coal fired plants at the time. Some ideas included more effective emissions control, which I thought would present the best opportunities for my technology but other discussions and pressure from environmentalists pushed for the elimination of coal as an energy source altogether. Which side would prevail was dependent on the political administration in power at the time. Republicans wanted less interference with production by the Environmental Protection Agency while Democrats wanted more control and some even the elimination of coal as a source of energy at all.

As administrations changed back and forth and changing a large power plant took a lot of time and money, there was a hesitance to do anything to fix emissions until a particular policy became the norm. They were anxiously engaged in unrealistic thinking or just ducking the inevitable and wishing the problem would go away. Whenever politics is involved, there is never a norm. It appeared that bureaucracies are largely made up of egotistic administrators who are more interested in peer acceptance, authority and dominion than in fixing problems.

It was in this uncertain environment that I made an effort to fix emissions by the use of the DMV. I was still in R&D mode and didn't have the capital without the participation of a large utility or a government grant. I learned that utility companies all over the United States each made contributions to a research arm called The Electric Power Research Institute (EPRI) at the time and I was advised by power companies to work through them. It was standard protocol for the development of any new technologies to be applied to the power industry. The protocol seemed reasonable on its face but for a new idea that was produced by an individual such as myself that was not directly connected or a part of EPRI was politically ignored because of what I came to know as the NIH factor (not invented here). It soon became clear that I was not going to get the attention of EPRI.

While persisting on the track of finding a way to apply hydropermutation to coal fired power plants, I met with the Chief Operations Officer of City Utilities in Springfield Missouri. The public utility was planning the construction of a new 300 megawatt coal fired power plant at the time to supplement their existing 270 megawatt plant to supply additional electrical power to meet increasing demand. Their funding appeal was for $1 million per megawatt, $300 million to build the plant, 1/3 of which was designated for emissions control, $100 million just to prevent the discharge of harmful particles and gases into the atmosphere. I wondered who had given them the quote but I was never told. I knew I could have done it with hydropermutation for 1/10 of that amount and made a significant fortune doing it and I explained that to the managers. Although they were intrigued with the idea, it seemed to them too good to be true and political pressure and pressure from the *"world class"* corporations in the business, they were unable to turn their heads. It was a huge political machine.

Convincing management in the face of global corporate powers that had command of the emissions control industries worldwide and also the recognition of political leaders because of their influence and notoriety, was of course futile on my part. Although I had the interest of the local utility management team, their interest was not enough to sway the emissions control method my way and the applications for permits had to be made with previously recognized methods instead. The problem with this attitude is that new ideas are stifled, innovation cannot help with the problem and the public continues to suffer with polluted air and high utility costs.

Coal is still the most plentiful known source of fuel for energy production. Known coal reserves have been estimated to be plentiful enough to provide 300 years of the total energy requirement for the United States. Before the year 2000 more than 50% of the electricity used in the United States was generated by coal fired power plants. By 2015 that number had dropped to about 33% due to the increased production of natural gas that has been produced by high pressure fracking in gas wells in fields across the nation.

The biggest influence on the decrease in coal use has been airborne exhaust emissions. Environmental pressure and the political influence toward alternative energy has caused a rapid move away from the use of coal as an energy source. In the same manner that rocket science won the day over flying into outer space by jet aircraft or by using the supergun technology being developed at the time by Gerald V. Bull to launch satellites into space, a popular trend supported by environmentalists brought about the political pressure necessary to move research and support into alternative energy such as wind and solar. Natural gas, creating less harmful emission than coal, became a step in the trend. However, fracking to produce more natural gas has come under controversy because of the problems of its creation of ground water contamination and other adverse peripheral effects to communities and property owners outside of the well sites.

Coal may come back and it could come back if big corporations and the globalist elite would allow it. Protecting their self-aggrandizing agendas is in the way of innovation. There is no technological reason for emissions from coal fired plants to stand in the way of burning coal. Global companies like Siemens, Monsanto and Wheelabrator have captured and held emission control innovation at bay to protect their business models, their antiquated technologies and the huge profits that they make by exploiting the environmental trend in the world. When an investment of$millions in primitive technologies has been made, primitive technologies are being sold to the power industry for a million dollars per megawatt. To abandon such a trend for the sake of any technology that cleans air ten times better for 10% of the cost would have an impact on them that could put them out of business. In view of that condition, they put their lobbying machines into high gear to convince political regimes and the public that they have the only possible answers for emissions control. Politicians were easy to convince because they believed that under the Keynesian system, a change to cheaper methods would effect the economy in a negative way.

Capitalism has worked for the the phenomenal growth and improvement in lifestyles, particularly in the United States. However when capitalist corporations become so powerful that they can either squash or buy out competitive or invasive technologies and do so, progress and mass life style improvement comes to a halt. There is no status quo in a capitalist system, When growth stops, profits diminish, jobs are lost and life styles suffer but it is only in the short term and only for the people that work for that company. When new technologies are allowed to make things easier and improve the environment and the overall health of the people, life styles of the masses are naturally enhanced in the long term and the world becomes clean energy sufficient and a better place to live. The problem is getting it past the barriers of the corporate government establishment. As time goes by, these obstacles become bigger and more ominous until finally there is an inevitable implosion of the establishment on a world wide scale.

CHAPTER SIX

NATURE'S WAY

UNDERSTANDING HOW GOD DOES THIS STUFF

The atmosphere of the earth is made up of several essential elements, among them are nitrogen, oxygen, carbon dioxide. There are others but these three will suffice for the purpose of this chapter. Plants and animals are dependent on these three elements for existence. Nitrogen provides a separation medium, or carrier for the even dispersion and distribution of oxygen and carbon dioxide. A cooperative balance is created between the plants and animals of the earth. Animals use oxygen, venting carbon dioxide as a byproduct and plants use carbon dioxide, venting oxygen as a byproduct. This creates a harmonious balance of the atmospheric elements that are essential for the existence of life on the earth.

There is a common misconception, largely by the tree-hugger segment of the environmental protest movement that elements can be eliminated. Elements are eternally existent and cannot be eliminated. This is quite commonly misunderstood. Elements do not convert into other elements. Rather, they associate or dissociate with other elements in different ways to create different applications and effects. For instance, the carbon taken from carbon dioxide by a plant is not converted into a different substance called sugar. It is associated with water to become organic compounds called carbohydrates or hydrates of carbon. Carbohydrates are a compound of carbon, hydrogen and oxygen. Sugar is simply formed as a crystalline form of carbohydrate, a compound of the original elements, not because any of the elements of the substance have been eliminated or destroyed.

By a process set in motion by the energy of the sun, plants on the surface of the earth absorb carbon dioxide. Then a phenomenal process takes place. The plant, by photosynthesis, will dissociate the carbon and the oxygen, keeping the carbon and venting the oxygen as a useless byproduct. Plants keep the carbon taken from the atmosphere in the form of cellulose which is an organic compound consisting of carbon and water. Cellulose makes up the body of the plant. If you remove the water from the body of the plant, what you have left is carbon. Wood is carbon derived from the dissociation of carbon and oxygen from CO2 in the atmosphere. As the tree grows it saves a great deal of carbon forming its trunk and branches that can be used by humanity as fuel to create energy. Other substances of carbon, such as coal and petroleum are also commonly burned to produce heat and energy.

Using a common and enduring procedure for obtaining warmth and light, a tree will be cut into blocks in preparation for use as firewood. Man has found by experience that it is hard to start a large block of firewood afire without first cutting it into small pieces. In fact, the smaller the better in order to start a fire. If the wood is cut into tiny pieces and dehydrated, it will become combustible by only a spark from striking a piece of flint against a steel object. Many fires were started in this manner before the invention and availability of the phosphoric match. It was also found that blowing on the tiny fire would help it to get going better. That is because the fire would not burn without oxygen and blowing on the fire simply adds more oxygen so combustion can be enhanced and increased.

So, what is happening when the fire is burning? The carbon and the oxygen are simply reassociating; they are coming back together again. This process of coming back together is a violent energy producing process called combustion. The gas produced by combustion of carbon with oxygen is carbon dioxide once again and the energy created by this process is simply the returning of the energy taken from the sun and used to dissociate the carbon from the oxygen by the plants in the first place. A great deal of unburned hydrocarbons and particulates are also discharged into the atmosphere by the burning process. Some of these particles are quite large and high in population and others can be sub-micron in size.

Elements are wonderful and cooperative too. The same process as burning wood is true with the burning of all carbonaceous substances such as the products of petroleum or coal. The combustion of petroleum, biomass and coal has created a great concern that the earth will be warmed and the environment damaged by the greenhouse effect created by the dumping of excess amounts of carbon dioxide into the atmosphere in the process of creating energy, chemicals or useful products such as steel or cement. Whether or not this is really a problem remains in controversy. Plants need carbon dioxide and cannot survive without it. Animals need the oxygen produced by plants to survive as well.

There is another harmful result that occurs peripherally to the process of reassociating carbon and oxygen by fire. Nearly 80% of the air that is provided to make the fire burn is not oxygen and does not enhance a combustion process. Air is 80% nitrogen. It is the nitrogen that previously provided the dispersion and distribution of oxygen and other elements in the atmosphere. Nitrogen is not combustible so what is happening to all of that nitrogen that is put through a combustion process? If you live in or around a city, look out your window and what do you see? That haze is called photochemical smog which is a combination of NOx or oxides of nitrogen, volatile (unstable) organic compounds and non-combustible particles called particulates. NOx is the nitrogen that has been heated, not burned, in the process of creating energy. Now it has been oxidized and is left over in various compounds, lingering in the atmosphere after the oxygen has been used for combustion and is re-associated with nitrogen and carbon to form carbon dioxide once again.

Water is natures scrubbing mechanism. Water is a most fascinating and versatile substance, probably more versatile than any other substance. It is certainly the best solvent known to man. Water is formed by the association of hydrogen and oxygen in a most cooperative relationship.

Having spent years studying atmospheric chemistry and pollutants I became very familiar with water and the water molecule. What wondrous things God hath wrought. A water molecule is a polar molecule meaning that it has both a positive and a negative charge like a magnet. Water, H_2O, is made of two elements, hydrogen and oxygen. The elements are held together in what is known as the hydrogen bond. As as magnets, positive attracts negative and repels positive and vice versa. The hydrogen elements are positive and the oxygen element is negative so they attract one another. There are two hydrogen particles clinging to one oxygen particle that is much larger than the hydrogen particles.

What is most interesting is that because they repel one another the hydrogen particles are clinging to the oxygen particle $104.5°$ apart. There is a very important purpose in the behavior of a body of water for this configuration. If they were only $90°$ apart or less, the particles would tend to attach themselves to the same oxygen particle. Since they are further apart than $90°$, each of the hydrogens will cling to separate oxygen particles thereby making the molecules attach in chains and creating the familiar surface tension that holds water together and makes it want to ball up when it is dripped onto a hard surface. As Nobel Prize winning physicist, Richard Feynman pointed out, *"all of the particles are trying to get inside the droplet."*

Have you ever taken a shower in an enclosed bathroom with the sun shining through the bathroom window and noticed that water droplets were visible in the sunbeam independent of one another? Did you wonder why the droplets floating around in the air do not come together and fall to the floor leaving dry air behind? Well, perhaps not but let me tell you why they don't. Since the water molecule is a polar molecule, the hydrogen is all pointing inside the tiny water droplets leaving only negative oxygen at the surfaces of the droplets. Because negative repels negative, the droplets are repelling one another, holding them apart in the air. This also happens in the atmosphere.

The surface of any sized body of water, from the oceans to the tiniest droplet, is negatively charged oxygen. This is caused by the hydrogen atoms all trying to get inside the water body, leaving the little oxygen butts of the water molecule sticking out at the surface. Since the surfaces of water droplets are all negatively charged oxygen, droplets suspended in the atmosphere are repelling one another. If this were not so, they would all come together immediately into one body and fall to the ground in one big splash instead of being evenly distributed in the air such as in a cloud. Water will remain in this parted state until a droplet is attracted to and contacts a substrate, usually a positive carbon particle. Because most things are made of carbon, whether live biological particles like bacteria and mold spores or common dust, The water molecules that have risen from the oceans, lakes and streams into the atmosphere by evaporation will attach themselves to the carbon particles and grow in volume until gravity delivers them back to the earth as raindrops, hail or snow flakes.

It was reported in the New York Times in 2010 that Dr. David Sands at Montana State University had found that bacteria like lactobacillus fermentum, or pseudomonus syringae are found in 70% of the snow crystals examined in samples from around the world, demonstrating that such bacteria are probably necessary for the formation of raindrops and snowflakes that fall from the sky to the earth. When bacteria that multiplies on the surfaces of plants is blown by the wind into the atmosphere, they go very high because they are very small and very light. Gravity has little influence on them. As they rise higher and higher into the atmosphere the pressure goes lower and lower. In fact, at 10,000 feet above sea level the pressure is about 1/3 less than at sea level and the temperature is below freezing. So when the water molecules rise from the surface of the earth to high altitude they are not liquid anymore but are ice crystals. The pressure that keeps particles from colliding in the atmosphere close to the earth's surface is alleviated at high altitude and the particles are less restricted from coming together.

Water can be more effectively used in smaller and smaller droplet sizes. The smaller the better for the collection of particulates from the atmosphere. Substrates for the accumulation of water molecules are provided by tiny particles that are suspended in the atmosphere, blown there by the wind to a very high altitude. How high they go is relative to their size and weight, the smallest particles being carried to a higher altitude than the larger ones. Then, because of its negative polarity, the outer surface of a water droplet, or ice crystal in the case of the low pressure at high altitude, will attach itself to just about any particle and relax, allowing the hydrogen atoms to stick out and become available to attract the surfaces of other negatively charged solid or liquid water molecules. When the droplets join in this manner, they become larger and larger until a raindrop is formed. The raindrops soon fall by the force of gravity back to the surface of the earth, delivering the substrate particle with them, thus removing the particles from the air and cleaning the atmosphere.

It can be surmised from these discoveries that the depletion of trees and plants around the globe upon which these common bacteria are generated could contribute to drought if these tiny bacteria nuclei are essential for the formation of rain drops. Dust particles and bacteria suspended in the atmosphere are the substrates upon which negatively charged water molecules accumulate. In fact, if it weren't for such particles and bacteria distributed in the atmosphere, it probably wouldn't rain very much, if at all. Effective scrubbing for the removal of particulates from localized atmospheres or emissions can be collected by the same method as occurs naturally in the atmosphere. Mechanically duplicating this natural process is the ultimate scrubbing technology.

Filters such as baghouses and others are essential and are used to intercept large particles that are undesirably discharged into any atmosphere, whether indoor or outdoor. They are the best means for eliminating dust, heavy particle loading and larger particulates. However, to finish the job, that is to stop the emission of particles smaller than approximately 10 microns in diameter that normally pass through filter media, a more effective technique needs to be applied, using the same method as nature. This can be accomplished by applying the knowledge we have of pressure differentials and electromagnetic principles in a more effective manner and by applying additional thermodynamics to the mix.

Duplicating the effects of nature's method of cleaning the earth's atmosphere can be accomplished continuously and instantaneously by the proper application of mechanical means. Using the energy that is required to transfer an air or exhaust stream and applying the three legs of thermodynamics; pressure, temperature and humidity, the scrubbing of any airstream to near zero particulate, including radioactive particulate emissions can be accomplished in an effective and efficient manner. Soluble gases such as sulfur dioxide, nitrogen dioxide and fluoride can also be collected in this same manner and in the same process, using nature's most effective solvent, sub-micron water molecules and droplets as the filter mechanism.

Electrostatic precipitation (ESP) has become an effective means of collecting particles by the application of an electrical charge that will attract oppositely charged particles from an airstream to a plate. By aligning several electrically charged plates within a housing and passing the airstream containing the particles through the grid and past the plates, particles are attracted to attach themselves to the plates in a process called electrophoresis, thus electrostatically removing them from the passing airstream. The process is largely effected by particle size distribution and particle resistivity. It is also negatively effected by decreasing polar attraction created by increasing distance in the airstream between the particles and the collection plates. A similar phenomenon can be observed in a similar device such as a battery or in a fuel cell where shorter distance between plates creates more separation of hydrogen from oxygen as the distance between plates decreases and the transfer of electrical energy is less restricted. Increasing the effectiveness of electrostatic precipitation devices is offset by increased energy requirement and decreased airflow.

Wet electrostatic precipitation (WESP) is the application of water to the process and using the water as an enhancement by applying the principles herein previously described in addition to the electrophoresis process. WESP is more effective for the collection of submicron particles and soluble gases. However, caking and cleaning can be more of a problem, depending on the nature and composition of particles being collected.

As with all other filtration mechanisms, there is a limit to the performance of both ESP and WESP because the distance between plates can only be reduced to a certain degree whereupon the flow rate decreases and energy requirement increases proportionately to a point where collection of particles smaller than 2.5 microns requires too much energy and cleaning up after collection becomes nearly impossible because the sub-micron particles imbed themselves in the porous surfaces of the steel plates. Maintenance and replacement costs are also a factor. The higher the effectiveness of the system, the higher the maintenance costs and the more rapid the replacement of the system. There is a need for a more efficient finishing system to meet the requirements of bacteria and particulate removal from the atmospheres created by energy production and associated with food handling processes. Nature's way is the best way.

Smoke is one of the most difficult emissions to remove from an airstream because of the high population of extremely small particles. However, if it is oily smoke it can be emulsified with water and captured very effectively. The trick is in the water/oil contacting mechanism. Particles will not be captured unless they collide with a solid or liquid surface provided by the collection mechanism.

Overcrowding and high population of the particles in smoke make it very hard for the tiny, nearly weightless particles to get through the crowd and contact a collection mechanism. WESP works better than dry ESP systems because the addition of water provides more surfaces for the substrate particles to come in contact with but it falls short of bringing all of the particles and water droplets together.

It is becoming more important for filtration experts to recognize that gases are particles too. Gas particles are molecular and have not heretofore been widely treated by the filtration industries as particles because filters cannot be designed to collect particles smaller than about 0.3 microns in size. The chemistry is effected by the the degree of willingness or compatibility of molecules to share electrons with other liquids or gases. For this reason some gases are water soluble and some are not. Soluble gases, such as sulfur dioxide are easier to capture with water than insoluble gases such as oxides of nitrogen. For instance NO2 is quite soluble while the rest of the nitrogen oxide group such as NO or NO3 is not. The empirical tests of the DMV there was a 20% reduction in NOX. The DMV was apparently capturing the NO2.

The same is true of odors. Alcohol based odors are easy to capture with a water mechanism while mercaptans such as methane or H2S gases are not. However, incorporating odorous substances with scavenger chemicals or alcohol in either solution or a homogenous colloid can provide a better capture mechanism for difficult odors. If all of this sounds too complicated, it really is not that hard to do with the right knowhow and equipment. Corporations just don't have the ears to hear when their business models are being invaded by new ideas or technologies. Those persons who are sycophants on a corporate ladder are not listening for alternatives. Hearing is largely prevented by pride, money, laziness, fear, egos, cronyism and a huge "*not invented here*" factor.

Wind and solar are championed by some to be the wave of the future for energy production. Hydrologic energy production from dams has been moved away from for surface environmental reasons. These all have their limitations. Wind power is what is called by utility companies "*dirty power*", not because it is environmentally dirty, although it may kill some birds, but because it fluctuates with the wind and does not produce power on a consistent and continuous basis. Solar is the same. It fluctuates with the exposure to the sun. Solar power is also restrained by the need for backup batteries that are environmentally dangerous and hard to provide because of the scarcity of lithium and other components required to produce them as well as the problem of disposing of them after use. These alternative power production methods are only a stopgap between fossil fuels and the power of water for energy and for a cleaner, healthier environment in the future.

CHAPTER SEVEN

ENERGY FROM WATER

NOT THE RUN OF THE MILL FUEL CELL TECHNOLOGY

Let me first qualify myself so that you will know that I did not just fall off of a turnip truck with a radical new idea. I have had more than 30 years of experience, since 1985 with environmental chemistry, experimentation and testing of the affects of applying submicron water droplets to the capture of submicron particles and harmful gases from the atmosphere without using filter media. My findings are proven true and correct and have been in use for some time now. So, now I come up with this ridiculous idea that water will burn without a fuel cell or electrolysis, C'mon man!

Don't believe everything you read on Wikipedia. Here is a powerful quote from Wikipedia with many references and notes to defend a position, a voluminous, complicated yet feeble attempt to keep the truth from an ignorant public. It was obviously written by an indoctrinated sycophant with an interest to protect in the petroleum and/or hot fusion industries:

"A water-fuelled car is an automobile that hypothetically derives its energy directly from water. Water-fuelled cars have been the subject of numerous international patents, newspaper and popular science magazine articles, local television news coverage,

and websites. The claims for these devices have been found to be pseudoscience and some were found to be tied to investment frauds. These vehicles may be claimed to produce fuel from water on board with no other energy input, or may be a hybrid claiming to derive some of its energy from water in addition to a conventional source (such as gasoline). Water is fully oxidized hydrogen. Hydrogen itself is a high-energy, flammable substance, but its useful energy is released when water is formed. Water will not burn. The process of electrolysis can split water into hydrogen and oxygen, but it takes as much energy to take apart a water molecule as was released when the hydrogen was oxidized to form water. In fact, some energy would be lost in converting water to hydrogen and then burning the hydrogen because some waste heat would always be produced in the conversions. Releasing chemical energy from water, in excess or in equal proportion to the energy required to facilitate such production, would therefore violate the first or second law of thermodynamics".

Not true! It would be true if the rules of thermodynamics were without error but there is a problem. Too many independent inventors have found opposing results. So, who are the real pseudoscientists?

Two professors, Martin Fleishman from the University of Southhampton in England and Stanley Pons at the University of Utah, announced in 1989 that they had discovered a way to produce energy from water at room temperature. The idea became known as *"cold fusion"*. The first experience with cold fusion occurred in Salt Lake City, Utah. After finding more energy out than was put in, called *"excess energy"* they disclosed to academia and the federal government that they had produced evidence that tends toward the invalidation of what is known as the second rule of thermodynamics whereas more energy is produced from water than the energy required to produce it. Meanwhile, Steven Jones of Brigham Young University had been working on what he called *"muon-catalyzed fusion"* and had been published in the Scientific American magazine in July 1987. Jones and Fleishman were discussing their work with one another along the way and had apparently agreed to publish their works simultaneously. However, the University if Utah, wanting first preference, pressured Pons and Fleishman to publish their works ahead of Jones in the Journal of Electroanalytical Chemistry. An application was then filed for funding to the United States Department of Energy by Pons and Fleishman in 1988 but it was declined. Why?

George H. W. Bush was the newly elected President of the United States at the time of the disclosure of cold fusion to the federal government in 1989 and Glenn Seaborg, the Energy Secretary, was the head of the Atomic Energy Commission. Both Bush and Seaborg had personal reasons to resist such an energy alternative as cold fusion and they also had strong institutional reasons not to believe it might work and to have it debunked, let alone funded.

Although Bush was personally in the petroleum energy business, Seaborg probably had the biggest ego to protect. Billions of dollars had been funded by government and spent by the *"hot fusion"* community that such an alternative as cold fusion could break down their whole house, their high station and even their very livelihoods. Academia had by that time become very dependent on the funds that had been provided for their research on nuclear fission. Much like the global warming craze, taxpayers had been funding their research for decades, to say nothing for the loss of pride and sense of purpose for the many professors and students that had dedicated themselves to its development.

Both Bush and Seborg had very high conflicts of interest. So when Seaborg met with President Bush in April, 1989 about the cold fusion issue, he told the President in his words, *"You can't just go out and say it (cold fusion) is invalid. You have to select a high level panel to study it for six months and they will say it is not valid, and that's what I did."* Of course, the high level panel was selected from a cadre of hot fusion advocates that had devoted their careers to the exact opposite technology. It would not be the first time *"free energy"* would be put away for the sake of money and special interest. J. P. Morgan put away the idea of hydrogen from water at the turn of the 20th century in favor of petroleum because he saw no money in it. Water was too plentiful and it was free. He could not fund such a project as water for energy when it was clear that there would be no return on an investment.

Cold fusion was also discredited by the scientific community of journalists who continuously published the opinions of the *"high level"* panel as fact. Opinions are not facts until proven. This was a huge step toward a news media that would head down the track of fake news and the reporting of false flags as facts without sufficient evidence to support their stories. The media reporters were reporting only what was edited by their owners and what they were being told by other special interests whom they perceived to be the *"important people"* in the world. They were deliberately ignoring and actively discrediting the other sides of important questions. Mainstream media and scientific publications became a propaganda dispensing machine.

Dangerous as it was, nuclear energy, like rocket science and global warming, got the attention and the funding for its development. The personal interests of Bush would be masked and protected and there would still be a lot of money to be made by the Bush family and others in the petroleum industry. The truth was suppressed and the liars would prevail for some time to come. Pons and Fleishman, discouraged and mistrusting of the United States government, left the country and moved to France to continue their research and consulting for other scientific applications.

Science writer, Eugene Mallove, and others at Massachusetts Institute of Technology (MIT), the most prestigious university in the nation for science, had experienced an excess energy result from their replications of the Pons and Fleishman experiments but, according to Mallove, the graph at MIT, showing the real result was overlaid by a plain water experiment, the true result was suppressed and the negative result was put forth as true findings. Mallove later resigned from MIT because of what he disappointedly saw as fraudulent behavior by the institution that he had so greatly respected. Meanwhile, Texas A&M University and others were finding verification of excess energy in their replications but their findings were overridden by the shoutings of Bush and Seaborg's "*high level panel*" of experts and in the scientific media publications.

Recognizing that a desired outcome tends to compromise the true data in research, I have always opted for the truth over the purpose of getting gain from any invention even though it is hard to make a living without sufficient gain to pay the bills. If I speculate on any of the points I cover here, it is because I do not yet fully understand everything about it. In fact, the more I learn about science and the elements, the more I realize that there is a lot of error and I have much more to learn than I have already learned. I also recognize that you do too and I am willing and eager to share so here we go! These are the things that I do know:

One gallon of common water, such as from your garden hose, a river, a lake or even the ocean contains the equivalent energy of many gallons of regular gasoline. Economical production of energy from water may be realistically available in the very near future if you, or someone like you, make it happen. I will show you here that it is not that hard to do. It can be done in your car, pickup or even your diesel truck with very few changes or modifications.

Did you know that the very first internal combustion engine vehicle, invented and built by Francois Isaac de Rivaz in 1805 was powered by hydrogen from water? There have been many patents issued for energy from water, many of them in the late 19th century after Rivaz 1805 invention. John Worrell Keely in 1872, who evidently inspired the work of Nicola Tesla; Henry M. Paine, 1884, whose system closely resembled the Pons and Fleishman device used for their cold fusion experiments; British inventors, William and Thomas Hawkins, 1893; Luther Wattles, U.S inventor, 1893; Inventors Eldridge, Clark and Blum, 1898, and others. The work continued in the early 20th century and onward, several patents having been filed to this day. Henry "Dad" Garrett, the inventor of radio communications for policemen in 1920 and the traffic light in Dallas, Texas in 1921, also invented a water for fuel method and demonstrated it on an internal combustion engine. An interesting account of a presentation to J.P. Morgan by Nicola Tesla on how to harvest free energy from the atmosphere was reported by James A. Robey, curator of the Kentucky Water Fuel Museum. It is said that Tesla's suggestion was met by Morgan's question *"Where do you put the meter?"* Such thinking has kept the rich and powerful, global elite in control of energy and the economy to this day. I recommend Robey's book, *"Water Car"*, available online for those interested in the history of the development of energy from water.

The combustion of the components of water cannot and will not cause pollution because the reaction of combustion only reassociates the hydrogen and oxygen back into their original condition, pure water. It can also be recycled, to be used again and again for the production of energy and then returning to its original state. Would you be surprised to find out that the surface of the sun is really a huge ocean of water, and that the tremendous heat from its core is producing plasma energy at its surface, recycling the energy from water back to water, repeating the process over and over again? Well maybe so. I will leave it to your imagination and reasoning since I really don't know, it is only theory and I can't prove it to you yet.

It is well known that water could be an important energy source if the presently known energy required to dissociate its components were reduced. The energy requirement for dissociation of the elements of water can be lessened by reducing water bodies to sub-micron sizes and suspending them in an even dispersion, using non-miscible, flammable liquids as the suspension medium. The reduced water bodies would then be exposed to concentrated high temperature zones created by a conventional hot spark plug, laser or high pressure or other means where the hydrogen and oxygen in the water are dissociated and exploded along with the flammable liquid to create energy, thereby eliminating the need for dangerous hydrogen storage and reducing or eliminating harmful NOx and CO_2 emissions in the process. It's not all about clean air here but also about clean and free energy.

Pons and Fleishman used platinum and palladium metal catalysts to produce the results at colder temperatures than I recommend in this chapter. They experienced energy from water that they called "*cold fusion*". Although a catalyst may enhance the dissociation process by bringing the required temperature down, I don't think it is necessary for dissociation and combustion of water at temperatures of 950°F or more. There have been several methods tried, and some developed, for using water as fuel since the invention of the internal combustion engine. There are a multitude of Btu's of hydrogen energy contained in each gallon of water but the energy required to break it down and make use of that energy has been notoriously high and inefficient.

There are two known ways of separating the hydrogen from the oxygen in water, electrolysis and thermolysis. Electrolysis has been the most explored method and the most widely used (fuel cells) but the energy requirement for electrolysis has been shown to be too high for efficient separation of hydrogen by dissociation. However, before this disclosure there has been no method demonstrated that includes the reduction of the size of water bodies for exposure of more surface and less volume to effect more reactive electrical conductivity. Thermolysis has shown promise for separation. However, the energy requirement for this process has also been too high to generate enough heat for the process to occur with a cost effective result. The reason is that it has not been realized by science that the water has not been reduced to kindling like wood, making the energy required for ignition very small as well.

The problem that has yet to be solved is the problem of the high heat or electrical conductivity energy requirement. Conductivity through a large body of water, in excess of 20 microns in thickness or diameter, is restricted by the surface tension resistance that is created by the positive/negative polarity of the water molecules. Although electrical conductivity is high in water, the dissociation of the components is slow because of surface tension resistance. This problem has prevented the extraction and use of the hydrogen energy contained in water in an efficient manner.

In view of the fact that water is a substance consisting of two hydrogen molecules and one oxygen molecule held together by what is known as hydrogen bond, water retains its integrity by surface tension. Surface tension is created by the high polarity of the water molecule. The hydrogen atom is electropositive and it has a relatively high positive attraction to oxygen which is a highly electronegative atom. That is why water beads up on a hard surface and is attracted to a substrate. How does this relate to energy production? It is also why the hydrogen in water is not readily available for ignition.

The larger the body of water, the more energy is required to heat it or conduct electricity through it. The reverse is also true. The smaller the body of water, the less energy is required to heat it. Water will turn into steam at 212°F at one atmosphere pressure. When steam is formed from water it becomes a gas. However, the gas (steam) is still made up of water molecules that are not separated into its component parts of hydrogen and oxygen. When steam is passed over a bed of red hot coal, the heat from the coal will dissociate the components of water which will react with the carbon monoxide produced from the coal, producing water gas or *"town gas"* as it was known before and during the Second World War. Hitler's war machine was largely fueled by town gas produced from coal because Germany did not have access to a lot of petroleum at the time.

Water gas is a combination of hydrogen and carbon monoxide. The hydrogen is derived from the water, thermally dissociated by the high temperature of the coal. The small droplet size of the steam exposes the water to the hot coals in a fine droplet that is easily dissociated because of the reduction of droplet size and subsequent reduction of surface tension caused by creating more surface and less volume in the downsized water bodies.

Oil refineries use the Claus process for dissociating hydrogen from sulfur by heating hydrogen sulfide (H_2S) gas to approximately 950°F. At this temperature, the hydrogen and the sulfur dissociate and are separated into their component parts, hydrogen being taken and stored away from oxygen to prevent combustion and the sulfur component being accumulated as solid granules of elemental sulfur. An important difference in dissociation of hydrogen from sulfur is that surface tension, caused by the positive hydrogen bonding to negative oxygen is not a major factor in H_2S gas like it is in water (H_2O). However, in view of the fact that the autoignition temperature of hydrogen is about 950°F, which is identical to the temperature that releases hydrogen from sulfur, it is reasonable to expect that the first level of autoignition of hydrogen by thermolysis is most likely to be the same temperature that will dissociate hydrogen from oxygen as well. So, the obvious question that follows is, how do you heat water to 950°F without losing it to steam by boiling it at 212°F before it can happen?

According to Albert Einstein's work, there is actually enough energy in a liter of water to surpass the burning of many thousands of gallons of gasoline if it were made possible to have full use of the water. What does this say for the second rule of thermodynamics? More energy out than energy in? Come on. Everybody knows that is impossible, right? Not only wrong but dead wrong. It is only a myth, popularized by primitive industries such as fossil fuels and later methods such as hot fusion even though with hot fusion it cannot be intelligently explained away. It did not require a lot of energy put in to get the result of an enormous atomic explosion out with the atomic bomb. In relativity Einstein also concluded that matter and energy are interchangeable. For example, that can be quite simply demonstrated by the observance of the interchangeable behavior of the gas consisting of two elements, carbon and oxygen called carbon dioxide (CO_2).

When a tree is formed, the plant acquires CO_2 from the atmosphere and dissociates the component parts (carbon and oxygen) by using the energy of the sun and chlorophyl as a catalyst. The tree accumulates the carbon component in the form of cellulose (hydrated carbon) and discards the oxygen back into the atmosphere. The cellulose will not burn without oxygen. The oxygen required for familiar combustion processes is acquired from the atmosphere where it was originally placed by the tree when it was formed.

The re-association of carbon and oxygen when carbon is burned produces a tremendous amount of energy which is exactly equivalent to the energy required to dissociate the two elements by photosynthesis. Deriving energy by burning carbonaceous substances such as wood, coal or petroleum is simply the completion of a chemical cycle. The fuel (carbon) is burned by re-associating the carbon (in this case wood) with the oxygen derived from the air and returning it to the atmosphere as carbon dioxide (CO_2) where it was originally acquired to create the tree, thus completing the cycle.

Water (H_2O), is an association of hydrogen and oxygen, much like the association of hydrogen and sulfur (H_2S) and the association of carbon and oxygen (CO_2). We know that the re-association of carbon and oxygen will produce energy as will the re-association of hydrogen and oxygen but first the components must be dissociated. In order for dissociation to occur with low energy requirement, the water needs to be divided into particles as fine as possible, making *"kindling"*, like wood. Tiny particles of water require much less energy for dissociation than visible quantities. This is true in both electrical and thermal processes. The amount of electricity required for dissociation of components of water by electrolysis is higher in large visible bodies than in sub-micron particles where conductivity is less restricted. The same applies to thermolysis. A common spark plug will produce the amount of electricity and/or heat required for electrical or thermal dissociation of the components of water when the water is made available in the form of sub-micron bodies. The use of a catalyst will lower the temperature requirement for dissociation to occur but a catalyst may not be necessary, nor more effective when the water is made available in small enough particles to be compatible with the small, high voltage, high temperature zones of spark plugs.

The re-association of hydrogen and oxygen (combustion) requires less heat than is required for dissociation so when enough heat is provided to separate the components, an explosion will occur, creating an immediate re-association of the hydrogen with the oxygen, and producing a great deal of usable energy in the process. The resulting re-association of the hydrogen and the oxygen results in the discharge of pure water which can be vented or recycled for reuse in the process. Perpetual motion, well maybe not quite, but whether or not it is perpetual recycling. Pure water is the most environmentally friendly substance on the earth, consequently, no pollution. So, how can we make use of this information?

In order for water particles to exist individually, they must be suspended in a medium such as air or liquid. Billings' U.S. patent #3,983,882 introduced the use of water vapor with hydrogen and air. This method requires that the water droplets be separated in a space containing air which is mostly comprised of nitrogen. Too much air. Since nitrogen is non-combustible, excess nitrogen will put the fire out. The most practical suspension for use as fuel is to suspend them in a nonmiscible, combustible substance such as kerosene, oil, diesel, biodiesel, vegetable oil, castor oil, mineral oil or gasoline because these substances are also flammable and will burn simultaneously with the hydrogen.

A small amount of any of these substances will provide a separation of the water particles in a homogenized emulsion that is sufficient to make them available for thermal dissociation in sub-micron form. A mechanical emulsifier or homogenizer will produce a suspension of these individual substances in the form of an emulsion that is tight enough to pass through a fuel filter and the injection system of an internal combustion engine without restriction. It will destroy a catalytic converter though.

Water bodies can be made smaller by homogenizing and suspending them with a nonmiscible fluid such as vegetable oil or petroleum products by the use of homogenizing or emulsifying means. Homogenizing the oil or gasoline with water creates a separation of the water droplets or particles into suspended fine bodies that can be readily dissociated by small concentrations of electrical energy and/or heat that are produced by a conventional spark plug or by the heat created by high compression.

The homogenized emulsion, when subjected to these small electrical heat zones result in a dissociation of the hydrogen and oxygen in the sub-micron water particles and they will combust and produce energy. After combustion has occurred, there is a re-association of the atoms, returning them to water in the same manner that carbon and oxygen re-associate when carbon is burned, reforming CO_2. The dissociation of H_2O will occur in varying degrees. Generally speaking, the hotter the spark plug and the smaller the water droplets, the more complete the dissociation of the hydrogen from the oxygen and the more effective the use of water as fuel. This can be practiced until a conduction level is reached that will dissociate 100% of the water into its combustible component parts, hydrogen and oxygen.

The finer the H_2O droplet size, the lower the energy requirement to dissociate its components. The more complete the dissociation of the water components, the less ambient air required for combustion because the oxygen required for combustion is provided in the water. Since ambient air is made up of approximately 80% nitrogen, a non combustible element, the production of photochemical smog (NOx) can be greatly reduced or perhaps even eliminated by burning the H_2O in a homogenized emulsion of non miscible oil and water.

Next question, can water be burned in a diesel engine that creates combustion without spark plugs? The answer is yes with enough of the friction heat created by running the engine along with enough compression to create 950°F at the top of the piston chamber. The autoignition temperature of diesel is about 450°F so the compression in the pistons of the diesel engine auto ignite the fuel without a spark plug. The heat of the engine, caused by friction will increase the temperature in the cylinders much higher than the temperature needed to auto ignite the diesel. When the temperature of the engine reaches 950°F, water injected into the engine as fuel in sub-micron droplets will automatically dissociate the hydrogen and the oxygen, creating an instant plasma ignition without the need of a spark to ignite it.

In the 2nd World War, water was injected into internal combustion gasoline powered engines, particularly aircraft, to achieve more power. Water injection was useful for particular situations such as getting heavy aircraft off the runway or helping fighter planes to fly out of a bad position in a dogfight. The general opinion of how the additional power was achieved has been that water, when heated to 212°F, will boil into steam that is commonly referred to as a gas, although it is not really a gas but microscopic droplets that go airborne. When water boils into steam, it expands to about 15 times its original volume and has been believed to, and probably does, increase the engine piston pressure, thereby boosting the power of the engine. Nobody thought that there could possibly be some combustion of hydrogen from the water in the process at that time.

I spent some time in Utah with Pete Schmidt, a highly respected diesel mechanic who bolted two V8 diesel engines together in an old truck in and set the one time land speed record for a diesel truck on the Bonneville Salt Flats at 258 mph. I asked Pete to tell me about the experience. He told me that his engine pyrometer was showing a temperature of 1750°F. Since steel melts at about 2200°F he was worried about melting the engine down so he injected water into the fuel to cool the engine. An interesting thing happened. He said that the driver told him that he could sure tell when the water hit the engine because it was like somebody had kicked him in the ass and he accelerated much faster down the track. I asked Pete what he thought was happening and he told me the same story that was commonly used to explain the extra power experienced in the 2nd World War. I then told him that *"my research had shown that if his pyrometer was reading 1750°F he was burning at least some hydrogen, I guarantee it"*. He was immediately interested.

Pete had a 671 six cylinder GMC diesel engine set independently on his back pad of his shop at his company, Utah Diesel at the time. I suggested that I would like to do a test to see if I could inject an emulsion of water and diesel fuel into the engine without plugging the fuel filter. He consented so I went back to my shop and mixed two gallons of emulsion with my DMV system, one with 20% water and one with 30% water and took them both back to Pete's shop.

We fired the stationary engine and injected the 20% emulsion with no problems with the fuel filter. The engine, being cold, hesitated at first and then smoothed out after about about a minute and burned the fuel without hesitance. We then injected the 30% water mixture having the same result after a longer period of hesitation before smoothing out. The engine was never completely heated to common operating temperature in these trials. Pete suggested that when an engine was heated to common working temperature, especially during the pulling of a load up a hill, the result would be enhanced and it was concluded that we would then be burning a lot of hydrogen.

Rudolph Gunnerman patented a process for burning emulsified water/diesel fuel in 1992 called *"Aqueous fuel for internal combustion engine and method of combustion"*, patent #5,156,114 that described the burning of a water diesel mixture like the mixture I created for the tests at Utah Diesel. I didn't know of Gunnerman's patent when we did the trials but I was refreshed to find that Gunnerman had been successful in burning the emulsified fuel in his experience as well. His method of dissociating the hydrogen and oxygen was by using a metal catalyst, perhaps learned from the Pons and Fleishman tests, and a surfactant to keep the emulsion from separating short term.

Gunnerman also suggested the use of alcohol in the fuel mixture. My research and experience shows that alcohol or ethanol is desirable more for the prevention of freezing the water fuel than for the enhancement of combustion. Common ethanol mixtures as much as 15% are now dispensed in the pumps at service stations. The ethanol will mix with water and prevent gas line freezing in temperatures as low as 15°F instead of the standard 32°F. Ethanol is recommended for any water/oil emulsion for this reason. Alcohol is not necessary to achieve the desired dissociation and combustion of the water. However, Gunnerman had come closer to the pure use of water for energy by thermolysis than anyone I had seen before and it has been proven by him and myself in repetition that thermolysis is better and more efficient than electrolysis and the popular, though inefficient fuel cell technology employed by many for the conversion of water to energy.

Gunnerman also used pre-emulsification of the fuel that required storage of the fuel before making it available to the engine. The problem with pre-mixing and storage of an emulsified fuel is that it separates over a short period of time and becomes useless because it will plug the fuel filter and the water will put the fire out. Storage of mixed fuel or the storage of hydrogen is not necessary with thermolysis because you can make the fuel mixture on demand as the engine requires it. The way to make an even tighter fuel emulsion with smaller more highly populated and wider dispersion of the water droplets for more effective and better efficiency of the combustion process is with a homogenizer valve. It is a common mechanism, the same process that is used to homogenize milk. Milk is homogenized to create a tighter dispersion of water and oil, in this case animal fat, droplets that will not separate short term which provides for a longer shelf life.

The temperature of the spark in a *NGK spark plug is approximately 932°F to 1472°F (500C to 800C), enough heat to dissociate the hydrogen from the oxygen in droplets as small as the spark. Thermolysis in these tiny zones can cause nearly 100% use of the hydrogen if they are all passed through the spark plug at the top of the chamber. This is because the finer the droplets, the less energy it takes to dissociate their components.

Homogenizing is accomplished by high pressure valves. The homogenizer valve can be adjusted for droplet size by a simple threaded screw to set the space the valve and the seat. The pressure required to operate the valve can be created by the addition of a second automotive power steering pump that is dedicated to the homogenization process. Power steering pumps normally produce enough high pressure to force the fluid through a homogenizer valve.

Gunnerman did not give a full explanation in the 1992 patent of what was happening in the engine with his water fuel mix. Probably because he did not have a clear understanding of the dissociation process at the time that the patent was applied for. He suggested that the use of a metal catalyst was the means of producing the dissociation of the hydrogen and oxygen. I have found that a catalyst is not necessary for dissociation if the temperature in the cylinder is equal to or above the auto-ignition temperature of hydrogen (950°F). Spark plugs, especially high performance spark plugs will achieve a temperature of as much as 1500°F in the tiny zone where the spark occurs. However, any standard spark plug will produce high enough temperature to dissociate the components in the water.

Type "*cold fusion plasma 9*" into your computer browser and watch a spark plug burning water. You will notice that the water is not being introduced in finer droplets than can be produced by a spray, the smallest of which will not be smaller than about 10 microns in diameter. Therefore all of the water is not being burned. Smaller droplets produced by your homogenizer will produce a better plasma and a more efficient use of all of the water.

A pre-mixer should be attached to the fuel tank to pre-mix the water and oil or fuel before it is introduced to the power steering pump and the homogenizer. There are options to accomplish that. You may want to attach a separate tank to pre-mix the fuel. You could use the factory installed tank to do this but if you do you will do away with the option of burning straight gasoline. Be creative and make choices that best represents your personal confidence and preferences. Practice will make it simpler.

The mixer can be constructed much cheaper than it can be bought from a mixer manufacturer. You can build your own mixer with a 7,000 rpm 12 volt DC motor that sells for less than $20 online and attach your own shaft and mixer blade to it with a small shaft coupler. You just need to devise a means of attaching the mixer motor to the pre-mix tank. Make the shaft long enough to extend into the tank about half way between the top and the bottom. A mixer attachment can be purchased online or perhaps at a mechanical hardware store. The mixer attachment will cause a vortex that will draw the oil or gasoline, which is lighter than water, down into the water and mix with it into a white liquid that looks a lot like milk. Don't be afraid to experiment with different impellers. If you find a better one, I would like to know about it. After pre-mixing, the liquid is ready for induction into the homogenizer valve.

Mount the mixer to the tank with a gasket to prevent leakage. The DC mixer motor will be activated by a circuit created by attaching wires to the 12 volt battery of the vehicle.

A power steering pump will provide adequate pressure to drive the pre-mixed fuel through the homogenizer valve. You will have to devise a mount for the pump that will attach to the motor block and line the pulley up with an existing pulley on the front of the motor. After it is attached and lined up, find a belt that will be long enough to run the additional pump with one of the devices pulling a drive from the front of the motor, perhaps the water pump or the existing power steering pump.

Buy the high pressure fuel lines needed to make the attachments from an auto parts store. Attach the intake fuel line to the pre-mix tank and from the outlet side of the pump to the homogenizer valve. Attach the Homogenizer valve outlet to the fuel rail to deliver the homogenized mixture to the engine.

The air line from the air cleaner filter chamber to the engine injectors doesn't need to be more than 2 inches in diameter. An adjustable control valve needs to be attached in the air intake line to be able to adjust the air to fuel mixture for optimum air to fuel ratio. You will adjust the air valve as the engine demands for smooth running and proper acceleration. At some point of the adjustment process it may be possible to eliminate the air intake line altogether, depending on the amount of oil or petroleum product is used in the mixture because supplementary oxygen from the atmosphere is only needed for the combustion of these carbonaceous liquids. It is yet to be determined but here is probably enough oxygen in the water to combust a substantial portion of these carbonaceous fluids. The carbonaceous fluids are only required in this application to provide independent suspension and dispersion of the tiny water droplets.

In tests of the DMV in South Korea in 2006, I was able to suspend the droplets with a very small amount of mineral oil in order to capture the airborne mineral oil mist in a copper plant. This test indicated that with a ratio of less than 10% of oil to water, the distribution of the droplets was sufficient to make the oil available to the air borne oil droplets that were passing through the machine. It can therefore be sensibly assumed that the droplets were made small enough in this test to be suspended in a high population and a thorough distribution in the fluid. The experience suggests that only a small amount of oil is needed to disperse the water in very fine droplets in the homogenizer. Additional experimentation and continuous operation is needed to establish the best optimums.

Oxygen is needed for combustion to occur regardless of the basic combustible material, gas or liquid. As illustrated in the previous chapter, ambient air contains about 20% oxygen. The rest of the air, except for a small fraction of other gases, is nitrogen. The only reason for using ambient air for combustion of the fuel in an engine is to make use of the oxygen in it. It has been found that an optimum air to fuel ratio for efficient internal combustion engine operation is about 14.7 parts air to 1 part of fuel. Since the oxygen needed for combustion in an engine burning water is already in the water, very little additional air, if any, is needed for the engine to run efficiently on water. Gunnerman found that an optimum air to fuel ratio in his experiments was about 1.5 to 1. This demonstrates that he was certainly dissociating the water to a high degree, deriving the oxygen necessary for combustion from the water and burning the hydrogen.

If you are motor savvy and know how to turn nuts and bolts and make things fit, you can do this. People have asked me why I have not patented this method. The answer is that I did file a provisional patent on it in 2014 but after a year, I abandoned it in favor of putting it out to the grass roots people of the world. I don't care if you live in Europe, Asia, the middle east, Africa, Australia, Russia or the United States. I truly believe that it is time that free thinking people have the means to free themselves from the oppression caused by the handful of huge corporations and that includes those in the nuclear and oil industries. I will do everything that I can to help you make it happen. If you have questions you can contact me by email at garry@enforcefreedom.com.

This is not about money, it is about freedom, personal responsibility and self reliance. God does not want you to fail! If you choose to exploit these methods to make money, more power to you but you owe me nothing. I advise you to do a thorough patent search before commercialization though. It is always advisable to respect the intellectual property of others. and you could get into trouble with the inventor and the USPTO if you don't. However, I think it is a great way to contribute to the grass roots economy. Your call. I would love to see you make it happen for the freedom and independence of mankind! Go out and save the world from the clutches of the corporate government establishment and save a lot of money doing it! Just don't try, like Pons and Fleischman, to do it expecting the support of the academic, corporate, government complex or you will surely fail.

CHAPTER EIGHT

THE AIR FILTRATION MENTALITY

DON'T CONFOUND ME WITH FACTS WHEN MY MIND IS MADE UP

It stands to reason that when confronted with a problem one will draw from experience and current understanding to solve it. Filtration has evolved in the realm of this mentality because it has heretofore seemed logical that if you want to capture smaller particles from an air stream, you must make the openings in the filter media small enough to capture them. Is there any other way known today to capture sub-micron particles from the air other than filtration? Nobody seemed interested in finding out how nature does it. The thought never even crossed the minds of the developers of new and better filters. They were probably in it for the money more than for solving the problem of dirty air. They could sell a lot of filters because filters would plug up and require replacement providing additional revenue when the user had to buy a new one and, even better, the tighter the filter the faster it would plug up and the sooner the customer would need a new one. HEPA filters are much more expensive than others and they have to be replaced more often. All the better for the revenue of the manufacturers and suppliers. It is called *"built in obsolescense"*.

There is an argument in the economics community that built in obsolescense is good for the economy because it keeps companies in business, keeps the money flowing and changing hands. When money doesn't move, stagnation sets in and the economy suffers. Companies cannot stay in business without selling products. Hence, innovation is impaired if it tends to replace an established product line because it may not just be solving a problem in a better way but it may also be causing companies to go out of business and jobs to become obsolete. This creates a tremendous amount of opposition to new, invasive ideas. Companies can change product lines but in most cases it is very upsetting and expensive. Companies do however adapt to new technologies after enduring a certain degree of pain. However, new technologies can eventually replace old antiquated habits, creating new jobs and new opportunities.

Filtration is like a fine screen. If the screen on the door will keep the insects out, a screen with smaller openings will keep the dust out too. Of course this is logical so the evolvement of filtration got its origin from screens. In order to stop the invasion of tiny particles it has seemed reasonable to create filters that would prevent the penetration of particles in the same way as screens stop the passing of insects through the screen door. So, engineering has spent a lot of energy and attention to the creation of tighter and tighter filters and new patents have been obtained for the improvements in the development of finer and finer screens, even membranes. Hence the origin of the HEPA filter.

The HEPA filter, *"high efficiency particulate air"* filter was first developed in the 1940s in conjunction with the Manhattan Project and the development of the atom bomb. There was a need for the prevention of small radio active particles from invading the atmosphere. The standard for HEPA filter efficiency was doctrinally established at 0.3 micron in diameter after it was declared that 0.3

micron was as small as most radio active particles and bacteria. The real reason was probably because that was as small as they could achieve with a filter. Besides, filter mesh so small that significant volumes of air cannot not pass through it and the energy to force air through such tight mesh is preventatively high. Logic and reasoning continuously demand a better way.

The restrictions of filtration must be replaced in order to capture particles smaller than 0.3 micron. Bacteria such as anthrax, are one to five microns in size. Bacteria have been classified to be between .03 micron to as large as 60 microns. Viruses are classified to be between .005 micron to 0.3 microns, exponentially smaller than the capacity of a HEPA to filter. To expect improvements in HEPA filtration technology to arrest viruses is impossible and logically out of the question. Dust particles have also been found in the atmosphere as small as 0.001 micron and they too cannot be captured by a HEPA filter.

Hospitals and pharmacies have been very cautious about the doctrine put out to the public having to do with the way diseases are transmitted. It has not been in the best interest of a hospital to allow the public to focus on airborne bacteria and viruses because such an understanding by the public would expose them to greater liability. The fact that nobody had yet developed a way to arrest airborne pathogens smaller than .03 micron with a filter stopped further development of filtration. Patients are told that staph infection and ebola viruses are not airborne but are carried on the skin of the patient. Such an impression, although largely misleading, tends to transfer the responsibility from the institution to the patient, even when it is not the most prominent source of virus invasions.

By applying a minor amount of logic, it can be easily be concluded that these harmful pathogens are definitely airborne because they are commonly found in the nostrils of the patients.

When a person coughs or sneezes, the aerosol produced is liquid droplets containing the bacteria and viruses. Although the droplets in a cough or a sneeze are classified between the size of 10 to 100 microns, much larger than the bacteria or viruses they have captured and contained. No wonder the virus and bacteria particles are found in the nostrils. These bacteria and viruses are vented to the atmosphere with the droplets in aerosols, thereby becoming available to other persons in the environment and spreading disease. Filtration will not capture these tiny particles to any significant degree.

The mentality and traditions of the public are not easily switched. Most people don't even think about such things, depending solely on the *"experts"* to figure it out and make it available to them. A common opposition to new ideas is the impression or argument *"if it can be done, why hasn't someone done it already?"* This mentality was purported to have closed the U.S. patent office in 1899 although it was only a joke and did not actually happen. The fact is that most people leave such complicated tasks to the scientists and prefer to carry on with whatever is available to them without changing anything. It appears to be easier that way although the truth, not indifference, is the way to make things easier. New innovations and ideas are the way to progress and improvement but resistance severely impairs the introduction of true solutions. Tradition is hard to break and filtration has been the tradition.

Tradition is ferociously defended by those companies that have invested huge amounts of revenue into the development and marketing of traditional products such as the HEPA filter. The fact that filters need to be replaced often, especially those with very small openings creates a huge market for replacement filters. Economists see this as a boon because it supports the necessity for money to keep moving through the economy on a continuous basis. A filterless air purification technique saves operators a lot of money by removing the need for replacement filters and discarding of the old ones. Filterless air cleaning also contributes to a cleaner environment by reducing the volume of waste and the related disposal costs. Uh oh, another job lost. Lost, or replaced? New technology creates new jobs but a paradigm shift will require re-training of workers. Not a bad thing but when someone or something moves your cheese, it is disturbing, so there tends to be a lot of resistance from the economists and the workers as well.

Air filtration may always have its place but it cannot perform the removal of sub-micron particles below 0.3 micron and cannot be depended on to remove viruses or allergens. There are a lot of harmful particles smaller than the performance limit of HEPA filters. The value of water as an air cleaning mechanism is more important than ever as the health community deals with viral infections and allergens being more and more prominent and recognized as a common cause of illness. The DMV becomes more important as the demands for cleaner air accelerates. That is the reason I have not been able to personally abandon the development regardless of the opposition against it.

With the exception of the common bag house, it is out of the question to use air filtration for the interception of the enormous population of particulates emitted from industrial smoke stacks. The particle count is so high in these kinds of emissions that a high efficiency filter would plug in a single day. Industries have turned almost exclusively to wet scrubbers and electrostatic precipitators to satisfy the demands of increasing regulations. These technologies have evolved much in the same manner as filtration, using improvements to existing methods to satisfy the demands of new regulations. Small improvements have resulted in new air quality permits for industries with emissions problems thereby keeping the trend alive and creating a stronger resistance to actually fixing the air pollution problem.

This was academic, political and corporate resistance to this monumental effort I found myself compelled to pursue. It had become clear that government regulation was not going to help accomplish cleaning the atmosphere. The three way dynamic kept passing the buck from one to another. Nobody was actually trying to find a real solution. They seemed more interested in pleasing or deceiving one another, whichever seemed to give them an economic or political advantage. The bureaucratic syndrome was to demonstrate power over industry and industry was doing all it could to dodge the government agency. It is not hard to understand why they would take that position over actually stopping the emissions at the tail pipe. They were afraid that if they did a better job than was currently required by EPA, they would raise the bar for compliance to a place where regulations would be harder to comply with. Besides, corporations don't like to be pushed around so barely complying, only because they were forced, to pacify the regulators became a more sensible tack for industry.

Tradition is also a most ominous obstacle that stands in the way of new ideas. Some truths take years, even generations to find acceptance and some never do find it in a world where pride, ego, greed and money are the norm. A powerful opposer of truth, and probably the most powerful of all, is the corporate and capitalistic process in a free society. Corporations are created for one purpose only and that is to make money for the stockholders. Corporations have to continue to grow and produce revenue or they fizzle and dissolve. This atmosphere creates an extreme pressure for the company and its employees to perform or lose their jobs. In America it appears to become the American dream for those that depend on jobs to sustain their lifestyles.

Global corporate influence stifles the introduction of new technology, no matter how superior it might be, in the interest of protecting the mighty international corporation. Invasive ideas, even though proven are easily squashed by corporate power and political cronyism. I was pushed aside, even after convincing the management of the utility of the viability of my methods, the applicant for the permits, because of pressure from government, as influenced by corporate lobbyists. I was in so far over my head that I was denied even a breath of air even if it costed the public utility $90 million to ignore me. Rates would have to become even higher while the public continued to live in polluted air. Another ripoff of the American people for the sake of greedy corporate interests and political cronyism. I was learning the hard way, coming to the realization that as long as they could keep me broke and pacified with false hope, I would never be a threat to their businesses.

It has been said that all is fair in love and war. Another leg could be added in the corporate world, one that employees will compromise moral principals in order for them to protect their jobs and qualify for promotion and a raise. The corporate world naturally evolves into the philosophy that all is fair in love, war and also in business. Lying and deception becomes what crosses the mind of the natural man, a necessary evil in order to protect ones job, after all incomes are necessary to sustain families and pay the bills. Tell customers whatever it takes to close a sale, even if it is not exactly true. Lie a little when necessary, the end will justify the means, a hollowed out approach from the outset.

No effort based on lies and deception can possibly last forever. It will inevitably implode at some point. Yet it tends to become the norm in this temporal, economics driven society. The attitude of loyal, yet conscientious employees becomes something like *"just get me through this job with enough money to support me and my family and I will be OK"*. I understand that forced compromise is a seemingly necessary mentality, I just never had the aptitude for it. A compromising attitude may be cooperative but it is a boil on the tail of progress.

CHAPTER NINE

THE KOREAN CONNECTION

SMOKE BOMBS, COPPER, BULLETS, COINAGE AND OIL VAPOR

Testing in South Korea in 2006 led to naming the device a Dynamic Multi-Venturi (DMV). I was introduced to Park Sang Eon by the company he was employed by in New York. The company he worked for was a relatively well known emissions control company that had established itself in South Korea as well as other places in the world. Park was their representative in South Korea. He had heard about my technology from his employer who urged me to work with him. He contacted me in 2005, wanting to know more about my scrubbing method with the intention of using it in his country. I was reluctant to extend myself that far at that point but I eventually told him that if he would file a patent for a different version of my device in both our names in South Korea patent office, I would disclose the process in cooperation with him and pursue its use in his country. I wrote the patent application, made drawings of the different configurations and sent it all to him. He filed the patent and the Korean patent was granted in February of 2006 and printed in the Korean language.

A demonstration was set up with Poongsan to scrub the emissions that were being introduced to a dry electrostatic precipitator(ESP) from a copper plant. The ESP was discharging a lot of dioxins into the atmosphere that had been generated by the high heat generated in the copper refining process. In temperatures above 1,600°F dioxins, like NOx are created to a high degree. According to the U.S. Environmental Protection Agency, Dioxins are highly toxic and can cause cancer, reproductive and developmental problems, damage to the immune system, and can interfere with hormones. The object was to scrub the emissions prior to their introduction to the ESP and eliminate the discharge of this toxic compound into the atmosphere.

Park then set up a date for me to come to Seoul, Korea for the testing and for the manufacture of a prototype of the Korean version with a partner he had arranged to own manufacturing and distribution. I went to Seoul that summer, a contract was signed and I stayed for a month while we designed and built the prototype for demonstration at potential customers facilities. I told him up front that I was skeptical of his position with Beltran, the company he worked for because the DMV would likely displace the application of their Wet Electrostatic Precipitator technology (WESP) in some of the applications. He assured me that it would not be a problem but I was still not convinced. Dongi Jong was the owner of the company that contracted the development of the Korean product. I liked Dongi Jong a lot and it was a pleasure to work with him. Park Sang Eon spoke english but Dongi Jong did not and I did not speak Korean.

After constructing the Korean prototype according to my specifications and design, tests were run in the company shop in Seoul. The Koreans produced a large smoke bomb the size of a small coffee can and introduced the smoke into the inlet of the DMV. The machine turned the water to look like paint the color of the smoke and there was still some residual discharge from the stack of the separator vessel. No instruments were used to measure the degree of removal but after some conversation via the translations by Park, it was finally realized that the percentage of airborne smoke particulate that had been captured by the DMV was very high. It appeared to be a start for DMV in South Korea and China and I was encouraged once again.

Upon request from Park and necessary shipping arrangements, I sent a small version of the DMV that I had had manufactured in Arkansas to South Korea for testing. Demonstrations were then arranged by Park with an international Korean company called Poongsan on the south end of the Korean peninsula in a highly populated industrial area. Air pollution was everywhere. As we stepped from Dongi's car, I heard Park sniff the air and exclaim in english "*mmm, air pollution, smells like money*". While the tests were being conducted, the environmental engineer employed by the company asked Park and me to walk with him to an enclosed area of the plant where mineral oil was being used as a coolant for the reduction in thickness of copper sheets and some for the extrusion of copper tubing. He was wondering if the DMV would arrest the vapor that was being released into the air of the work environment from the machines in the plant.

A slip stream was set up upon my recommendation to vacuum oil vapor laden air from the roll press with the DMV and scrub the emission into the water in the DMV separation tank. On the day of the test Park and the engineer were reluctant for me to mix oil into the scrubber water so I cooperated with their request. It failed to arrest the airborne oil. On the way to the lunch room at noon, I placed my hand on Dongi's back and said in English "*Mickey Mouse now, Mighty Mouse later*". He didn't speak english but he knew what I was saying. He had heard of both of those American cartoon characters. He grinned back at me.

After lunch, ignoring the early reluctance, I picked up a ladle that was by the machine and caught a small amount, less than a cup, of oil from the drain on the press and began pouring it into an access port on the DMV. They looked at me with curiosity, wondering what I was doing. The oil immediately turned the ten gallons or so of water in the separation tank as white as printer paper and the oil vapor discharge at the top of the separator ceased. As I had expected, the oil vapor had been captured by the oil droplets into the scrubber liquid. I could see that the engineer, who did not speak english was puzzled by what had happened so I went to him and wrote on a paper in english, oil + water = emulsion - oil + oil = absorption. He nodded that he understood and immediately to Park and me on another tour of the plant, showing the locations where he would like to place the DMV vapor capturing systems.

I met Butch Otter in 1986 when he was running for Lieutenant Governor of the State of Idaho. Butch was the only son in law of J.R. Simplot, the Idaho potato tycoon who had established a corporation from scratch that became the country's largest private corporation. His only daughter, Gay Simplot was married to Butch Otter before Butch parted company with Simplot Corporation for business reasons. Now he was in politics. I, as his Fremont County Campaign Coordinator, wrote a campaign song for him and the other republicans that were running in the election. I sang the song at the republican rallies in the State. Twenty years later, I rewrote the song and campaigned again for his run for Governor of the State of Idaho. He won both elections.

I also met with the President and CEO of Simplot Corporation along with their Business Development manager. The meeting took place in a high class restaurant at the top of a hotel in Boise, Idaho. The subject was a consideration by Simplot for the takeover of the DMV technology for their own use and the development of a market to make it available to other companies. The only application of the DMV under consideration at the time was emissions control. While considering the menu, I was asked about my food preference. My reply was that *I was not concerned much with the menu, I was like the cowboy that went to the wedding party, tasted the caviar and loudly declared that there was something the matter with this jam*". The ice was broken and we had a very nice conversation about my technology.

Toward the end of the meeting, the business development manager declared that Simplot would take over my technology but they could not promise me anything. I took that to mean that I would not be included in the technology development process, nor could I expect to be paid at any time in the future so, at the end of the meeting I told them thanks for lunch, left and did not look back. Looking back, I think I missed an opportunity. Terms could probably have been worked out that would have included me in the development and future profits. It also could have accelerated the marketing and use of the technology.

As time passed, more applications were to be discovered that were outside of the interests and business model of Simplot Corporation. The agricultural application for pathogen removal and disease control, which could have benefitted Simplot potato growers to a great degree, was yet to be recognized. It did not begin until 2011, twenty four years later.

After Butch Otter was elected Governor of Idaho, a meeting was arranged with the Idaho Department of Commerce (IDC). That meeting began a relationship that led to a meeting at the Governor's house with South Korean business leaders and, the following year, a trip to South Korea with the IDC for promoting business relations between South Korea and the businesses of the State of Idaho. At the Governor's house, I met Jin Roy Rhu, the President and CEO of Poongsan, a Korean company that re-processed copper, manufacturing ammunition and is the world's largest producer of coin blanks, producing coinage for 70 countries, including the United States. He brought a friend with him who spoke at the conference, Colin Powell, former National Security Advisor for Ronald Reagan and the U.S. Secretary of State in the George W. Bush administration. I met and talked with Colin Powell about what I was doing with technology but I didn't expect that he would help me with it. Jin Rhu gave me a recently coined Thomas Jefferson Dollar as a gift that day.

At the meetings on Jeju Island off the southern coast of South Korea a year later, I met with Jin Roy Rhu again. At that meeting, he asked me if I was leaving from Seoul with the IDC the next day. I told him that I was staying an additional day. He then set up for me to make a presentation in Seoul the next day and called his plant managers from plants in locations all over South Korea to attend the presentation. I asked Park Sang Eon to be at the meeting for translation purposes which I found to be a mistake. Park had not been properly prepared for the presentation. The presentation did not go very well and I felt like I had fallen short. I have since talked with Jin Rhu by telephone in an attempt to revive the interest and go forward with providing the technology for his plants around the world but I did not have the resources or the capital to meet the company at the level required to make it happen. Little, under capitalized people cannot compete in a world market. Big companies play with one another. Little guys are most often not accepted if they lack the resources to play, regardless of the value of their technology.

A recent report from Park, my Korean partner indicated that Poongsan is still living with the oil vapor in the environment of their copper plant. Dongi Jong gave up. His company too was also too small to compete or endure the long periods of time required to get a project together. Once again and still, I was diminished to a voice crying in the wilderness. I have kept contact with Park ever since and there has been some movement this year, 2017, toward reviving the effort with a South Korean partner, this time with a finished product manufactured in the United States.

CHAPTER TEN

DREAMING CAN BE DANGEROUS

CREATIVITY DEMANDS MORE THAN IMAGINATION

In 1991, I arranged for a slip stream test of the DMV on an oil refinery in Woods Cross, Utah. The results of the test showed a great deal of removal of the sulfur dioxide (SO2) from the refinery exhaust. The owner was excited about the results and determined to move forward with a project until the disposal of the residual sludge from the process became an issue with the water side of the EPA and the state. There was a conflict between air and water departments in the regulatory process. When the horror stories of sludge disposal regulations came to the attention of the refinery manager, he abandoned the idea of cleaning the emission in favor of whatever he could do to avoid the direct attention of the EPA.

Nineteen years later, the same manager, now with his own independent oil refining company, began talking with me about using the DMV for recovering the oil vapors that were being emitted from the storage tanks on the refinery location. The customary process in all refineries was to deliver the tank vapors to a flare and burn them. The flares have become the identifying characteristic of oil refineries across the world. They all had them. I discussed the possibilities with him and made a trip with him to one of his refineries 65 miles west of Ely, Nevada, where he wanted to install a system. His desire was to mix the oil vapors back into the crude oil product if possible instead of using the flare.

I studied the possibilities of mixing the vapors with the crude oil and later informed him that I was not confident that I could do this because the methane molecules in the vapors would not cooperate. Methane molecules are very stable, having four legs of hydrogen attached to a single carbon atom and they were therefore not eager to share electrons with any other gases or substances. However, I explained to him, if you are willing to put in place a plan B which would be to vacuum off the tank vapors with the DMV and mix them with the refinery furnace fuel or the boiler, perhaps using the DMV to regulate the air to fuel ratio and deliver the mixture to the burners, I would be willing to provide him with a DMV machine. He bought on that premise and a year later and a DMV was manufactured and installed on the refinery.

After testing the mixing vapors into the crude idea and failing as I had predicted, a low profile became the next step for them. Although I was not aware at the time, the Nevada State Department of Environmental Quality (DEQ) was giving them more time after the installation of the DMV because it appeared to them that the company was trying to fix the emission problem. On my third startup visit to the refinery, being frustrated with the lack activity toward the exercise of Plan B, I asked the chemical engineer that had been assigned to the project if their intention was to fix the problem or to pacify the DEQ. His laughing reply was "*If the DEQ is pacified, we don't have a problem*". I knew at that point that I was done. I was also frustrated enough to leave behind any oil refinery pursuits because any business as small as I was could not live with the uncertain schedules that were regulated by unpredictable government control and speculative air quality permits.

After the Nevada oil refinery project was completed, or at least compromised, I met a man who had connections with a large geothermal power generation company that had geothermal power plants located at the Geysers north of Santa Rosa, in northern California. The company, Calpine, owned and operated 17 of the 19 geothermal power plants in the area. A very large concentration of H2S gas was coming up from the wells with the steam that was used to turn the generators. The H2S, being very dangerous to the environment was being treated the same as in oil refineries using heat to dissociate the sulfur from the hydrogen and collect it in a bin, thereby preventing the discharge of the H2S into the atmosphere in its dangerous and odorous form.

The problem Calpine was dealing with was a large component of mercury, also coming up with the steam and being incorporated with the sulfur. This problem caused the sulfur to not be allowed for commercial use but instead it had to be disposed of in a hazardous waste storage facility to meet environmental regulations, a procedure that was dangerous in handling and very expensive. The capture of airborne mercury had been previously demonstrated by the DMV, then called Hydrop, in work that had been done by the engineers in Pennsylvania, showing a 93% removal of airborne mercury in their tests.

I formed a company with the man and the team was joined by two other men in Idaho, one of them his brother, who were willing to pay for development of the process. The plan was to recover the mercury before it was introduced into the furnace and allowed to join with the sulfur after thermal dissociation. A proposal was made and accepted by Calpine to move forward with tests of the DMV for the continuous separation of the mercury in their process. My partners saw this as a get rich opportunity to make $millions over night. I did not see it that way. Dreaming is dangerous. Practicality overrides gluttony. However, it presented a potential for at least a couple of million dollars in business if we were to be successful in our trials.

There were approximately 40,000 ppm of H2S gas coming up with the steam from the geothermal wells, very dangerous since it only takes about 600 ppm to kill a man. The DMV had to be sealed and air tight before the safety team at the company would pass it for testing. This required special attention to detail that went beyond the ordinary operation of the machine, including valves and seals that were sure not to leak or fail. This was early October. The test date was set for December 13. We had to work fast. The system required a sealed bearing and fool proof valves and fittings used in the gas/ liquid separation stage in order to meet the safety specifications.

I went to work on the project but the new team didn't seem to take it as seriously as was needed to be ready for the demonstration. The budget was more limited than I had previously understood. On a return trip from northern California in his private airplane, one of the partners made me uncomfortable by telling me that his patent attorney in California, whom I had not previously been made aware of, had advised him that my patent could be broken. I was left with a suspicion that it might be his intention to ignore my intellectual property and go forward with the project without honoring my patent.

Meanwhile, the coordinating partner considered it more important for him to go hunting for a month in late October and early November, out of communication instead of getting ready for the demonstration. Another one of the three partners considered snow mobile trips with his friends to be more important than getting prepared. I struggled to get ready without the help of the others, personally hiring a man to help me and buying parts needed for the system within my limited capacity. When it was done and tested in house, it fell short of my comfort zone to meet the safety specifications. The machine was warped, causing the seal to leak and the cheap, off the shelf hardware and fixtures that I could personally afford were not adequate to be fail safe. I told the partners that, from a professional standpoint, I could not support a demonstration of the machine on the Calpine plant without better integrity of the system.

The hunting partner returned from his hunting trip and informed me that they were going to test at Calpine on December 13 with or without me. I immediately sent them a letter, informing them that if they continued using my patented technology without my support, I would file a patent infringement lawsuit against them. I also informed Calpine that I did not feel comfortable to support the demonstration on the designated date without further and better preparation. The partners, ignoring my warning, took the machine to the Geysers on the designated date without my support and were turned away for the lack of integrity in the machine. The project was discarded by Calpine without even hooking up for a demonstration or a test, a multi-million dollar project was lost because of neglect and incompetence.

The partners were given 30 days to answer my letter. They did not take me seriously and I heard nothing from them so I filed the complaint of patent infringement in the Federal District Court in Salt Lake City as I had warned. It cost them more than they could afford to defend the complaint. They had to hire a qualified attorney, practicing in patent law at the federal level, to defend the case. After negotiations with an independent engineer they designated for that purpose, I settled the case with no compensation to myself and a dissolution of the business arrangement or claims to the patent on their part. I did give them a license to pursue the application for use on coal fired power plants. They failed to develop the application and it was abandoned. The original partner, along with his two young daughters later died in a plane crash on February 26, 2017. I was very sad.

Pipe dreaming is a useless waste of mental energy. One of my colleagues accurately and adequately described it as "*mental masturbation*". I have found that the majority of people would rather spend their time dreaming than to get in the trenches and make something happen. I found that to be particularly true with gold prospectors. They loved to sit around the coffee shops and bars, talking among themselves of their claims, making believe they were rich, or at least massaging the idea that they were going to be.

To have a mining claim was a badge of honor in coffee shop conversations. Proving the claims was too much work for a good coffee shop or bar hand. Besides they might find out that their claims would turn out to be worthless. I was looking for real ore that could be refined and separated by my comminution and separation machines and I was always willing to share the profits in a win/win business arrangement. Sharing pipe dreams was a waste of my time and theirs. I was not successful in developing the business of custom milling and refining. For lack of qualified ore, it was a bad business model and my partner investors were not willing to switch the plan to the sale of equipment. That was 1984, before scrubbing became my focus.

I have been guilty of pipe dreaming, mostly in my youth. Considering the possibilities can be an adventure but it is usually riddled with erroneous thinking. I dreamed I could fly when I was a boy and actually envisioned myself flying around on my own in my dreams without any sort if device to help me do that. It felt good and free but of course, practicality in the familiar world made it impossible. It was only a dream. I have found myself considering possibilities quite often while contemplating a different way of doing something or considering an interesting business plan or arrangement. In a perfect world, you expect that all people would catch your vision and cooperate with all of your ideas. You expect that all things imagined could work if only they were to be applied in the right way. There are no holes in such dreams. They always seem sound until an obstacle is discovered, whereupon the dream must then be altered or done away with to fit the new practicality.

Putting dreams and imaginations into reality is a far greater challenge than just mere contemplation. Empirical application demands resources, determination, commitment and ambition; action far beyond the dream stage. This is where most projects are ended. Dreaming is fun and easy. Building a dream is more than can be withstood by an ordinary man, especially if the idea or thesis is generally unpopular. Creativity is one thing while actual creation is entirely another. Creation is painful and demanding. Peer pressure and cronyism have destroyed many a creative project.

Like crabs in a bucket, peers continually pull any person that reaches for the rim of the bucket with a new idea back into the bucket to remain with the others. To make a leap for the rim of the bucket is the ultimate treason. The crab that leaps for the rim and succeeds finds himself alone in an unfamiliar world supported only by his personal dream and without company or support. That is only the beginning of trouble. After abandoning the bucket, the adventure lies ahead and it is rife with pitfalls and barriers not yet imagined and that are yet to be experienced. The crab no longer looks like a common crab, he is something different, something that is yet to be discovered, even by himself and perhaps eventually even by the crabs that were left behind in the bucket.

In a college psychology text book, I once read a description of schizophrenia that intrigued me. A psychologist in England opined that schizophrenia is really a sane reaction to an insane world. In other words, crazy people simply opt out of society because they are being lied to, lied about, stolen from, abused verbally, emotionally or physically… or all of the above. They see the world around them as an ugly place to be so they drop out. They give up control and responsibility for their own lives and behavior. Many turn to alcohol and/or drugs to fill the lonely void. Many are homeless, destitute and paranoid.

I tend to agree with that psychologist's opinion because it makes sense to me but it brings up another thought for consideration - I see everybody around me dropping out on occasion, people take vacations to get away from the "rat race", drink coffee to wake up, alcohol to forget the work day, take drugs to temporarily relieve pain, anxiety or depression; or just to feel better for a little while; people get sick, get divorced, buy chocolate, cinnamon rolls, a fast car, a boat or a motorcycle, fix baldness, get a facelift, join a support group, or even go so far as to become homeless to avoid the responsibility of paying rent. Don't get me wrong. I don't intend to be hard on homeless and hopeless dreamers, just observant.

Considering the crazy world around us today, it isn't any wonder that people drop out, and they are doing it at all levels. The world appears to be out of control. Its like some crazy carnival ride, a carousel that never stops and it is impossible to get off short of suicide, and that option probably provides no relief. The devil we know may be better than the devil we don't know. The President and congress lie to us and we involuntarily pay them to do it. That isn't to say they are all crazy but sometimes I wonder, and I also wonder if we all might be a little bit crazy. I know we're certainly handicapped. Even the President makes mistakes. President of what?,,,, I leave it to you.

I was diagnosed with attention deficit disorder (ADD) when I was over 40 and I thought I was handicapped, so I took my prescribed Ritalin for awhile until I realized I was really in the company of some darned special people. Then I switched to vitamins on the advice of a good doctor and left the drugs behind. I have since come to realize that many accomplished achievers were probably ADD, like Churchill, Patton, Einstein, Buckminster Fuller and many others who didn't do well in school for lack of interest in subject material that seemed useless at the time and were sometimes prone to insubordination. WOW! My 6th grade teacher used to put me in the hall on multiple occasions, not because I was a bad boy after all, but just to get me out of her way so she could teach the class without my interference, yet I'm really a winner here? Now that's a handicap I can live with.

I love it! We are all mentally handicapped. Isn't that great! And guess what, we are all physically handicapped too. I have never met anybody who really had it all together. The blind, hearing impaired, autistic, artistic, athletic, proud, rich and famous ...... or broke and famous, there are a lot of those out there too. When you are rich or famous you are handicapped because you can't tell anyone you are broke or sick and its hard to tell the difference between your real friends and the ones who are just enamored with your iconic presence. Now, having met you, they can hardly wait to rush home and tell their friends. They say they love you but what they really love is how you have increased their attention getting ability in their own social circles. How do you tell the difference? That is a handicap and it can get darned lonesome in that condition. Uh..oh, bring on the feel good substances. Time to cry a little. Life confined to a wheel chair, blind or something might be easier in some ways than being rich or famous.

Beware of fame and fortune just as well as a life of struggle and poverty. They have their disadvantages too. There is always a price to pay, no matter the degree of achievement. So what? At some point sensibility has to trump the cop out or we all fail.

You know, this is really kind of exciting, to realize we are all handicapped in some way. (If you don't believe you are at this point just wait until you get a little older) . See how your bones feel then.

So we are all handicapped and crazy, now that makes sense. Now I can live a little longer in the rat race and feel OK about it. Sometimes the rats appear to be winning but that's just a test of my confidence and determination to be free, so I guess I won't drop out after all.

Vince Lombardi told his team in 1970 *"It's easy to have faith in yourself and have discipline when you're a winner, when you're number one. What you've got to have is faith and discipline when you're not a winner"*

In order to have contact and exposure with the Chemical Engineering Department at Idaho State University, I returned to college for a semester at the age of 52. While I was there I took a class on movie making. There was a text book and weekly assignments to watch a movie and write a revue. At the end of the semester, I delivered my final paper to the professor and he read it on the spot. His comment was: *"Interesting dichotomy here - why is it that you get A's on all of your papers and F's on all of your tests? "* My reply was *" The older I get and the more focused I become, the less apt I am to memorize useless information."* He said *"Oh, you mean you read the material but you don't commit it to memory? "* My answer was *"That's right, if I ever need the material, I know where to find it. It's in that book."* He gave me a final B grade for the course in spite of the fact I had flunked all of his tests.

Incidentally, knowing that I'm really OK, just handicapped and mentally handicapped, helps me sleep better, smile a lot, be nicer to people (even if they don't think I'm cute) and be confident enough to outstrip the depression and disappointments of the human condition without the supplements.....and with a clear head. *"Onward and upward"* as an old colleague used to say. The world is really not as bad as I used to think it was.

I think its a matter of choice. I can choose to take that pill, or I can feel better on my own. Well, I guess it doesn't work that way all of the time but I think if I choose to feel better on my own and practice a little bit, I can feel the pain less and get over it a little easier and faster and perhaps even permanently without all of the cop out supplements. I don't want to hurt, I don't want to be sad or depressed, But I don't want to be dependent on substances to preserve my well being. In short, I would like to be a better person. So, in spite of the crazy world things are always looking up.

Well we all know it isn't all that easy to change habits that have been around for awhile but I want to leave the thought with you that with the right attitude and a degree of determination, we can at least head in the right direction with the confidence in knowing that a goal is out there and it can be reached. A little improvement along the way represents success in itself. There are things that need to be stopped *"cold turkey"* or we can't move ahead. But it helps to know that It doesn't matter so much where we are today or how far we have come as it does where we are headed. I hope for me and all my family and friends that we are headed for freedom, more individual responsibility and for the Pollyanna Zone. I guarantee from my own experience that there is a large measure of happiness in the doing. Do something nice for somebody before the day is over. It will lift your spirit and make YOU feel better. It will also be a step toward finding the Zone.

CHAPTER ELEVEN

PRESERVING THE POTATO

"When you're one step ahead of the crowd you're a genius. When you're two steps ahead,you're a cra*ckpot*.

Rabbi Shlomo Riskin, (Feb. 1998)

Having spent my early life in the mountains of Idaho, I was exposed to the seed potato industry on many occasions and I was usually found sorting seed potatoes for income before the snow melted after a hard winter. My Father owned a sawmill and I mostly worked in or around the lumber industry but in the winter logging was shut down and winter work was scarce. The small wages earned by sorting and packing potatoes was welcomed by the time April rolled around. That was my first introduction to potato diseases. We were sorting out the rotten ones called culls. I never thought about what made them rot at the time and I didn't think about it much for years after that.

It wasn't until 2009 when I had moved to Utah again and was often spending time with Dennis Gifford, by now in his 70s, an old friend and potato farmer from my home town. He had been one of the seed potato growers around Ashton Idaho who had since retired and moved to Salt Lake City. He had had a stroke sometime in his '40s but it did not appear to shut down or impair his creative thinking. He talked a lot to me about potatoes and particularly about the diseases that caused them to pre-maturely deteriorate in storage before they were sold and shipped.

After harvest in the fall, potatoes were being stored through the winter in root cellar type structures for as long as 7 months before shipping them to commercial growers for planting in the spring. By the year 2009 the storages constructed were mostly above ground but many of the old storages were still in use by the seed growers. Potatoes were being stored in bulk and piled as high as 18 feet, filling the entire storage building from wall to wall for as far as 200 to 400 feet in length. Storages this large would contain as much as $1 million worth of potatoes in a single pile.

Dennis was a Democrat. I was mostly Republican, although I didn't take it as seriously as he did. He was from a family of Democrats with deep seated traditions, which commitment effected his approach to relationships with professional researchers. We didn't talk politics much but we had many discussions about potato preservation. With no credentials in chemistry or physics, he found it difficult to impossible to get the attention of professors and researchers, largely Democrats, who did. There is a profound resistance to any ideas that are not originated with the college, or other reputable colleges. No outsider with a new idea is to be considered if he does not have a degree related to the subject he is talking about, so he is pacified and largely ignored.

Dennis' interest was in a chemical disinfectant, specifically chlorine dioxide (CLO2). It wasn't a new idea but, though it had been tested, it was not being used for potatoes. It did have a popular application in the beer industry for disinfecting the equipment because it did not leave a residual odor or taste to the beer. After looking into the characteristics of CLO2, I could see that his theory, which was different, was probably correct. Chlorine dioxide is an extremely volatile gas that is produced by adding a low pH acid , generally phosphoric acid, to high pH sodium chlorite. Dennis' theory was that the acidic additive was not necessary to produce the reaction because the low pH amino acid that was contained in the potato would be enough to replace the sodium chlorite and produce the CLO2. I did some work on it and found that the pH of potatoes is 2 to 3 points lower that neutral. I began to think his theory was correct.

The reason CLO2 had not become a treatment of interest in potato preservation was that, in a gaseous condition after being activated, it was violently fugitive and distribution could not be controlled, much like ozone. Applying it Dennis' way would have prevented uncontrollable distribution, a problem that was letting the gas go free and everywhere until it was applied. He spent as lot of time and effort trying to get attention and being pacified by the Agricultural Extension division of the University of Idaho. The University, staffed by renowned potato experts as it were, was not interested in research that was being done outside of their customary procedure since their research was being funded by grants and their studies paid for by government and chemical companies. Dennis didn't have any money to contribute so, by virtue of the way things work, his research and theories had to be ignored for economic reasons. *"Money talks, BS walks"*, as they say. Even truth walks if it is being presented without money.

It was sad and frustrating for him because he knew he was on to something that might be very useful for potato growers. Too bad it was being stifled by chemical corporations such as DuPont, Dow Chemical and their distributors. Chemical manufacturers had spent $millions getting their products approved and labels for them, largely with the paid for support of universities like U of I, but they couldn't say so, so they pacified Dennis instead. Universities don't solve problems, they research them, if they are paid to do so. If a solution were to be found and a problem solved by the university research, it would put them out of the money and render them useless. Hence, all research findings and conclusions are summed up with a statement that more research needs to be done.

Dennis became so frustrated and angry that he began calling the professor who had been pacifying him "Dr. Dunce". The university legal department finally called him with threats to pursue legal means to shut him up . They had to protect their interests and their integrity. He shut up and became very discouraged, understandably so. Two years later he was dead.

Storage management techniques had evolved by then, mostly influenced by the advice of the ventilation companies and the chemical industry. As much as 2,200 cubic feet of air per minute per ton of potatoes in the storage was being recommended by the ventilation companies. This number had increased from a small amount of air recommended when under the pile ventilation tubes were first introduced about fifty years prior to 2010 and an air plenum began to be built into newly constructed storages to allow for circulation to be provided through the potato pile.

Potato and other vegetable storage facilities are largely controlled by ventilation systems trading outdoor air for indoor air as a method of reducing the population of airborne pathogens. However, there is a problem with using outdoor air that has not heretofore been adequately addressed, the bacteria and mold spore content of outdoor air. Berkley Laboratories in Berkeley, Calif., conducted research on the bacteria and microorganism content of outdoor air. This research had been conducted using a DNA method of identification instead of the usual surface colony count. This has enabled the lab to identify over 1,800 species of bacteria contained in ordinary outdoor air around two Texas cities.

The significance of these tests to the farming industry is that regardless of the location, outdoor air contains a great deal of bacteria, especially at harvest time in potato-growing areas. When crops are ripe and ready to be harvested, the bacteria and mold spore count is highest because they have been growing and multiplying throughout the growing season. Since they are microscopic and invisible to the human eye, they have been ignored and their presence has not been adequately recognized.

Potato storage facilities are usually bathed profusely with outdoor air in preparation for the harvested products to be put to bed for the season. This practice introduces every form of bacteria and mold contained in the ambient air to be available for multiplication on the potatoes injured at harvest. Many of the bacteria are not harmful; however, those that are harmful are guaranteed to be present, along with the rest, thanks to this profuse ventilation method. Hence, multiplication of harmful micro-organisms can begin, eventually promoting pathogenic activity such as soft rot, silver scurf and others.

When rot begins to develop in an area in a potato pile, the bacteria or fungi that promote the deterioration of the potatoes goes airborne, circulating by ventilation fans from place to place in the storage unit and becoming available to all of the potatoes in the storage facility. Hot spots begin to grow and produce more and more bacteria that is released into the air as they perform their designated duty to destroy potatoes. Unless checked, this bacteria is equipped to destroy an entire potato crop within a short period of time. As growers are fully aware, profits can be eaten away with just a little deterioration.

Fungi are great destroyers of potatoes. Fungals such as silver scurf, black dot, fusarium, pink rot and rhizoctonia can have profound effects on the profit line if left unchecked. When these harmful organisms are left on the potatoes, as any marketer knows, it makes them unacceptable or at least harder to sell and less attractive to the consumer.

In order to limit the multiplication of bacterial rot, a variety of companies, brands and labels of chemicals containing different ratios of the same two ingredients, peracetic (peroxyacetic) acid and hydrogen peroxide were commonly being applied to the stored products. Attempts were also being made to alleviate fungals such as silver scurf and black dot, the most common destroyer and cosmetic detriment of potatoes with the same chemicals. Consumers were turned off, or at least turned down by the appearance of mold on the potatoes in the produce departments of the grocery stores. Sales diminished.

When chemicals are introduced to the storage area in a fog, they are not distributed efficiently because the droplets are too heavy. The repelling affect of negative oxygen on the surfaces of water molecules in the ambient air keeps them apart for a time but as gravity takes effect on them, they fall from the atmosphere before they are distributed throughout the room air. Pressure differentials play a big part in preventing even and thorough application of chemicals to all areas of the potato pile. If chemicals are introduced in droplets larger than 10 microns in diameter into the ventilation system by a fogger, they are restricted to a point where they are not as effective as desired for sanitation. Gravity will pull the larger droplets to the floor instead of distributing them through the potato pile. Where there is no control of pressure differentials, distribution is restricted by the pressure in the ambient atmosphere.

In order to make the droplets small enough for better suspension in the air, thermal fogging is used by some applicators, using heat to create steam to provide smaller droplets that will stay airborne. The smaller droplets created by thermal fogging will distribute better through the potato pile, but additional facts should be considered as to the thermal effect on the chemicals being fogged:

1. Peracetic acid breaks down at temperatures above 60 degrees Celsius (140 degrees Fahrenheit).

2. Hydrogen peroxide dissociates at temperatures above 280°C (536°F).

3. Thermal foggers use air heated to 500° to 600°C (932° to 1,100°F).

Some have claimed that these chemicals are not in contact with the heat in a thermal fogger long enough to destroy them, but studies have shown that a residence time of less than one-half second will destroy peracetic acid. At any rate, a grower should ask himself, "Why inject chemicals with heat if there is even a chance that they will be limited in effectiveness if it is not necessary?"

Studies have found that as a post harvest sterilant for apples and pears, peracetic (peroxyacetic) acid caused increased damage from fungi This was possibly because it killed microbials on the surfaces that were antagonistic to the pathogens. Peracetic acid, the main active ingredient in many popular and approved disinfectant chemicals, actually caused increased damage from fungal rots. Could this also be true in potatoes, causing an increased infestation of silver scurf and other fungal agents such as fusarium, black dot, early blight, pink rot, powdery scab or rhizoctonia? Where is the data to support that this is not happening?

So, how can these problems be fixed? If the air could be scrubbed and the microorganisms removed prior to entering the storage area, the possibility of bacterial and fungal deterioration could be significantly reduced. This begs a few questions:

1. Is it possible to remove the pathogens from the storage air?

2. Can it be done economically?

3. Will it pay off in product sales and profits?

The answers to these questions and more can now be a resounding "yes" with the products such as the Dynamic Multi-Venturi (DMV) blower/scrubber/applicator, also known as the Humigator. Storage environments can now be totally controlled by a humigation system, including

- air transfer and circulation,

- constant removal of 99.65 percent of airborne microorganisms, and

- constant humidity maintenance without wetting walls and floors.

These functions can occur using far less air or water and less energy. To solve this problem the Humigator draws air from the area of the storage room, thereby creating a vacuum that will naturally be filled by the cleaned air delivered into the plenum. The air is continuously vacuumed into the inlet of the Humigator, where the airborne pathogens are captured into the scrubber fluid (water) and the cleaned air is discharged into the storage area and made available to fill the vacuum created by the suction. If clean, humid air is vacuumed through the pile by removing the pathogens and regulating and controlling the pressure differentials in the pile, disease reduction is assured and infestation of healthy potatoes can be eliminated.

Potatoes are sold by weight. Weight loss is directly related to profit and it can represent as much as a 15% reduction or more of the bottom line. Pressure bruise, largely the result of dehydration of the tubers also decreases the value of the potatoes. Experts have discovered that disease such as silver scurf can also contribute to dehydration, shrink and weight loss. Silver scurf and other fungi grow rapidly on wet surfaces.

"Silver scurf, (a most common disease of potatoes) may have a transient effect on potato growth and tuber yield" (Mooi, 1968; Denner et al., 1997). "The light brown lesions (silver scurf) increase the permeability of the tuber skin causing shrinkage/water loss and therefore weight loss" (Hunger & McIntyre, 1979; Read & Hide, 1984).

Relative humidity (RH) is the amount of water contained in air relative to the air temperature. It is measured by checking the difference between dry bulb and wet bulb temperatures of the air. Water content of potatoes in storage is directly related to the water content of the storage air. Dry air causes potato weight loss because the moisture is drawn out of potatoes toward an equilibrium with the water content of the storage air. Potato storage air should constantly be maintained between 95% and 99% RH at all times if possible to limit pressure bruise and to keep potatoes from shrinking by dehydration.

"If weight loss is compared over six months of storage at various RH levels, potatoes stored at 90% RH could lose 9% in weight, or nearly twice as much weight as those stored at 95% RH. Given a storage capacity of 100,000 cwt, and a value of $5.00 per cwt, the building maintained at 90% RH would return $22,000 less than the storage controlled at 95% RH. The impact of maintaining the proper RH cannot be overstated." *Nora Olsen, University of Idaho Extension, potato storage specialist*

It is important for storage managers to understand that at 64° F, the air will only hold about 15 grams of water per cubic meter of air space (0.42 grams of water per cubic foot of air). As the temperature drops, the air will hold less and less water. At 42° F, the atmosphere only holds about 5.5 grams of water per cubic meter of air space (0.155 grams of water per cubic foot of air). Air at 53°F will contain almost twice as much water (10.4 grams per cubic meter) than air at

42°F (5.5 grams per cubic meter).

For instance, a storage building, 60 ft by 150 ft and 18 ft high contains 162,000 cubic feet or about 4,576 cubic meters of air space. A gallon of water weighs about 3785 grams. Total water saturation of the air space of this empty building at 42° Fahrenheit would be achieved with only a total of about 6.65 gallons of water. If the air space remaining after a building is full of potatoes is 25%, the total amount of water that the air space will hold at 42°F is less than 2 gallons (1.66). If more water could be added to the air space, it would leave the air and things would begin to get wet. Cold surfaces on building walls or beams will also lower humidity by condensation. This causes the drip lines commonly seen below the beams of a storage bin. Whenever condensation happens, the air in the storage is giving up water and is becoming drier. The colder the air, the drier the air and the more potatoes will shrink.

Water droplets produced by atomizers that are large enough to be seen with the naked eye are of no use to humidify the air except for the small percentage that evaporates by temperature differential. They may look very small to the eye but in order to be seen, they must be larger than 10 to 20 microns in diameter. Droplets this big stay suspended for a time and then fall with gravity to the floor or attach themselves to tubers, the ceiling and the walls. Standing water, wet tubers and other surfaces invite the growth of diseases such as silver scurf, black dot and rotting.

Potatoes are refrigerated to prevent the multiplication of harmful pathogens. Swamp cooler (wetted fabric) type refrigeration systems produce a great deal of excess water. Wet fabric, floors and standing water provide a breeding ground for pathogens. When the temperature rises above 41™ F pathogenic organisms begin to grow and multiply - even at 45™ F (just 4 degrees warmer), bacteria grow 10 times as fast as they do at 41™ F.

Airborne bacteria and mold spores were eliminated from the environment by the Humigator, leaving clean, healthy potatoes available for the market and for human consumption. It was a good start but the opposition was still there and very active, using their influence to scorn Humigation as a crackpot technology based on pseudo science or on no science at all. The chemical distribution companies that had been trying to stop the spread of disease by periodical disinfectant chemical applications were fighting the technology for obvious reasons. If the pathogens were to be removed from the storage environment, there would be no need, or at least not as much need for their fungicides or disinfectant chemicals.

DMV, by now named "Humigator" for vegetable storage preservation had now been proven to remove pathogens from the air as it is circulated in the storage facility. The system began to be used by several growers and has since been successful in preserving their potatoes without the use of chemicals. Humid air, produced by a Humigator™ after pathogen removal is dispensed in small enough water particles to be invisible to the eye and to remain airborne. With continuous operation, Humigation without humidity suppression has proven for potato storages to maintain humidity at 95% to 99% RH, just below condensation (dewpoint), without saturating the walls and floors of the plenums or the surfaces of any of the potatoes.

A good and simple gauge for checking humidity in a storage bin is to blow your breath through it. If you can see your breath at any temperature even though you don't see wet potatoes or surfaces, the RH of the air is between about 95% and 99%, right where you want it to be. To be able to do this throughout the storage season without wetting the plenum is particularly desirable since dry air shrinks potatoes and destructive pathogens need wet surfaces to grow. Good humidity control throughout the storage season contributes highly to substantial profit for the grower.

The automatic monitoring and control systems typically set up to control temperature and humidity in potato storage have been programmed by the suppliers of the equipment. Temperature is typically read into the system from thermocouple probes set strategically inside the storage area or the potato pile. Humigation® from Isaacs Hydro Tech is being used on an increasing number of potato storage buildings (cellars) since 2012. I have visited these cellars periodically throughout the storage season and have been monitoring the operation of the Humigation® process monthly throughout that storage season. Part of my routine has been to check humidity in the storage area using a sling psychrometer. Both wet bulb and dry bulb temperature readings are taken and the difference between the two indicates the humidity or water content relative to the temperature of the air in the cellar.

One cubic meter is equivalent to 35.31 cubic feet. 1 cubic meter of air at 30 degrees C can hold 30 grams of water As air cools it holds progressively less water, thus as 20° C it is just under 20 grams per cubic meter, and at 10° C it's closer to 8 grams per cubic meter. At 7.22°C (45° F) 1 cubic meter of air holds only about 6.5 grams of water. That translates to about 0.18 gram of water per cubic foot of air. Any amount above that will condense. That is why you can see your breath on a cold day.

Cold air is very dry. Dry air dehydrates potatoes, reduces weight and exacerbates pressure bruise. Once pressure bruise occurs, it is generally irreversible. That is why it is so important to keep the humidity as high as possible and the airborne pathogens removed during the healing period. Removing airborne pathogens in the process is a wise practice because that is when potatoes have most likely been injured by handling and are most subject to inoculation.

There is no reason to use more water than is necessary to keep the air saturated. Wetting floors and walls does not provide effective air humidification. It does however provides a place for pathogens (mold and bacteria) to grow and multiply. Humigator uses whatever amount of water it takes to keep the humidity as high as possible without condensation at any temperature plus approximately 10 gallons per week (whatever is dumped) during the healing period after digging and then reduced to about 10 gallons dumped monthly, after the initial air is clean and the potatoes have healed and are no longer being disturbed.

My periodical temperature readings have shown that temperatures are usually higher than growers think at the top of the pile. Since warm air rises, it would be expected that the temperature at the top would naturally be a little warmer than below but my readings have shown that from April through August, the temperature at the top of the pile is usually over 50° F in most of the storages I have checked.

Humigation® is primarily an airborne pathogen eliminator. Simple reasoning dictates that if 99.65% of pathogens are being constantly removed in a single pass from the storage atmosphere that the bacterial deterioration rate is certainly reduced or eliminated at any temperature. Potatoes have been kept in storage with Humigation® through the summer with high integrity. Part of this positive result is caused by keeping the cellar and plenum dry while keeping the humidity high. Russet Burbank potatoes have been kept at high integrity in 2013 until the 20th of August with no reduction in weight or integrity with Humigation.

Tradition has been that keeping the temperature below 50°F has been necessary in order to preserve food products from bacterial deterioration. Michael Thornton of University of Idaho Extension Service, Parma, Idaho has stated that if potatoes could be kept at temperatures over 50°F, fewer problems would be experienced in cooking and processing.

Potatoes kept under Humigation® have all maintained high integrity and appearance even at temperatures as high as 67° F. There were 10,000 cwt of a yellow variety being kept in Eastern Idaho at high integrity with no refrigeration through the summer of 2014. A Model 1225 Humigator was operating in the plenum 24/7. The temperature in the storage was as high as 67° F throughout the summer and the RH was at 95% plus. These potatoes were shipped disease free on September 20, one year after harvest. Indications are that potatoes can be kept healthy and better hydrated at higher temperatures when operating Humigation throughout the storage season.

It has now been proven that potatoes can be kept healthy by removing the airborne pathogens as opposed to keeping them cold enough by refrigeration to prevent the pathogens from rapidly multiplying. So, what can this technique do for other refrigerated products? Or, better yet, what can it do for the atmosphere in a home, school, hospital or office building/ At the time of this writing, experiments are expected to be conducted by Idaho State University Microbiology Department for further testing. Tests will be conducted through the summer of 2017. Research will be ongoing for some time to come. The reports will be publicized periodically on the internet for all to see.

The opposition to humigation grew. The University of Idaho had established itself above the other universities in the State to be the go to source of information and instruction in the potato industry in Idaho and also in the Northwest. Because Idaho was recognized to be at the cutting edge of potato production in the United States the influence of the University of Idaho was recognized worldwide as being experts in potato and onion production and storage. In keeping with the academic and government complex, the U of I research was largely funded by chemical companies that were using the university to establish the credibility of certain fungicides and disinfectant chemicals that they were developing and to obtain a label that allowed for them to legally distribute the chemicals on the market. The disease problems of potatoes in storage provided a substantial platform for much of this research and justified the funding of several research projects to be performed by the University by both corporate interests and by the government.

Not realizing how deep the chemical industry had established itself by financial support to the University at the time, I approached the lady professor in charge at the U of I research laboratory in Kimberly, Idaho with an offer to demonstrate a Humigator machine in her facility. The lady professor had become known as an expert in potato storage and she taught the annual potato school that occurred at Idaho State University in January each year, instructing potato growers on the best methods and techniques for successful potato storage and product preservation. Her instructions were naturally based on her experience with the testing that the University had done over many years of research done by the University and funded by government and the chemical companies that were interested in capturing a substantial portion of the potato industry market for their chemicals.

Not knowing how to hold off my offer to demonstrate the Humigator any longer, the professor accepted my offer to demonstrate the system at her facility. In the demonstration I showed her and her assistant how to humidify the air in a storage building without using excess water that wetted the walls of the air plenums and accumulated puddles of water on the floors. The professor in charge was so distracted that day with other things to do that she did not make herself available to observe the process for herself so she allowed her assistant do it for her. The assistant was impressed and recognized the benefits. What followed was continued ignorance of the technology by the Kimberly Laboratory and the University. In one of her potato schools, after three years of ignoring my system, I heard her say that the atomizers (spinners) that were being used to humidify the air in storages were great. The spinners were sold by the ventilation and chemical distribution companies.

I raised my hand and raised a question, "I heard you say spinners are great. Spinners put out 30 to 40 gallons of water per hour. The air in the storage full of potatoes will only hold 3 to 4 gallons of water before it becomes saturated. What is all of the extra water for?" She had obviously ignored my demonstration of 3 years prior to the school and she could not answer the question. I later found out that the establishment of the Kimberly Laboratory where she worked had been largely funded by Agri-Stor, a Blackfoot, Idaho chemical distribution company and I immediately recognized a conflict of interest for her. I had inadvertently placed her between a rock and a hard place. What was she to do? It was sad and frustrating. In an effort to get more answers and to find a way to be recognized, I contacted the Dean of the University of Idaho Agriculture Extension Service in Moscow, Idaho. He subsequently sent me a letter demanding that I refrain from contacting him or any of the University staff any more, so I stopped trying with them. Humigation began to feel like "cold fusion" must have felt to Pons and Fleishman when their research and findings , though being replicated by other universities, were opted out in favor of larger and more powerful interests.

Further information was yet to come. What I did not know at the time was that a patent had been filed by Phillip Wharton, assigned to the of the University of Idaho in 2011 and published in June 2015 named "Compositions and methods for inhibiting potato pathogens", Application number US 9044033 B2. The University of Idaho had a hidden agenda that would be hindered by any attention to an alternative pathogen control technology such a Humigation. I was on my own and in direct conflict with U of I Extension Service agenda. I had mistakenly thought that the University Extension Service had been created to help me to help the potato growers of my state. Like Pons and Fleishman before me, I had not anticipated that a conflict of interest would prevent me from being recognized by the academic government complex. In the mean time however, business was growing, customers were adopting the Humigators in seven US states and two provinces in Canada. I was compelled to do an end run around traditional methods of research and development. My customers helped with that with their individual willingness to give it a try.

Humidity was being distributed in as high percentage as possible for the potatoes but it had also being reduced to about 50% by the discharge system and duct work in order to create an ideal work climate for a school, hospital, work space or for a home. Healthy potatoes are wonderful but healthy humans are much more important.

Meanwhile, more grants were being applied for. In 2017, a federal $1.37 million grant was made to the University of Nevada through the National Science Foundation to investigate the molecular-genetics and biochemistry of potatoes, more specifically for the purpose of finding a better way to preserve potatoes in storage. Humigation was still running behind the research and recognized credibility curve. However, a grant was also being approved in 2017 for a cooperative research project with Boise State University, Idaho State University and IHT to find the capacity of Humigation for the collection of sub-micron particles, including mold spores, bacteria, allergens and viruses. When these tests are completed, a verification will be established for the cleaning of air at the greater depth and efficiency needed to prevent disease in humans. Finally, academic participation, the results of which are expected to turn the heads of the skeptics.

CHAPTER TWELVE

CLEAN AIR FOR HUMAN HEALTH AND SAFETY

WHICH ARE MORE IMPORTANT, HUMANS OR VEGETABLES

Contrary to popular belief, rain does not clean the atmosphere of the earth. Nature uses a cleaning mechanism that is totally different from filtration or wet scrubbing. No possible alternative to nature's method of air cleaning can possibly be better. To master the mechanical duplication of nature's way is the ultimate air cleaning technique. In this chapter I will open the possibilities of natural air cleaning to many different applications. Applications of naturally cleaned air can improve human health in a myriad of indoor environments such as hospitals, schools, office buildings, homes, work places etc.

The question was looming, how does humigation work to keep the indoor air clean? To answer that question, I will explain it so it can be recognized as real technology and not just a magic black box.

Airborne particulates including bacteria, fungal spores and objectionable odors enter the Humigator, a rotary device consisting of a water atomizing impeller housed in a unique enclosure that incorporates a patented, advanced geometric design. Fluid is injected into the airstream and the fan/impeller blades impact and accelerate the air and water droplets to create a dense aerosol of suspended fluid droplets. The aerosol is passed through several low-pressure venturi zones, causing them to associate in either solution or a compact colloid with bacteria and fungal particles to be collected by the water stream in a dynamic mixing process and collection chamber. No filter is required. Humigation constantly provides a net pressure increase instead of the significant pressure drop associated with venturi and electro-static scrubbers, substantially lowering operating costs.

Humans are suffering from environmental pollution more than at any other time in history. Industrial pollution is not the only source of air pollution although they are a major contributor. There are bacteria, mold and viruses that are airborne and in the atmosphere around us at all times. A large number of diseases are caused by invisible airborne pathogens such as bacteria, allergens, viruses and mold spores.

I was introduced to Missouri State University Chemical Engineering Department in 2004. After making a presentation on the technology to the Physics, Astronomy and Materials Science, the department head, Dr. Ryan Giedd asked me how my invention worked. As I explained its function to him, he became interested because of a research grant that had been funded by the U.S. Navy in association with the U.S. Department of Homeland Security that had been obtained by his department for the identification of anthrax in the air. He had no way to identify the anthrax without a way to capture it first. I told him that I could capture it but I would not kill it with my system which was exactly what he needed to do for the project. Over the period of about six months, I was placed on Adjunct Faculty at the University and I made three different machines for the project.

During my time at MSU, the name of the University was changed from Southwest Missouri State University (SMSU) to Missouri State University (MSU) in 2005. While serving on the adjunct faculty there, I wrote and presented an application for a National Science Foundation grant that was declined with a request to file again next year. I did not reapply. I was impatient and broke, so I moved on.

After many years of frustration and empirical experience, looking at several options, I learned that a significant reduction of sick leave alone from schools and offices is enough to offset the cost of installation and operation of a natural air purification system such as DMV. Finding financial support for making the DMV available to fix the problems caused by airborne viruses and bacteria had been impossible because of political and corporate power supporting traditional technologies. However, agriculture provided an alternative to corporate and political obstacles found in other industries. The loss of potatoes caused by diseases had not been effectively curtailed prior to the introduction of the Humigator. Agriculture opened the door for further development. Potato growers were looking for an answer for the losses of revenue caused by shrink and disease.

Colleges and universities have been at the heart of research and development. They are not significantly motivated to come up solutions and they are notoriously funded to do research and so research never ends. If it did, the college would no longer be in a position to continue its research. A trend has been created whereby students learn to depend solely on their professors and the text books they read. By this trend, a box is created, innovative thinking, by nature, ceases and most students leave the institution to work for established companies with business models that are built around company products.

Innovation and the development of new ideas is not commonly found in the companies they work for. When individuals within a company innovate, whatever they develops is claimed by the company they work for. They find that they have simply moved from one box to another and both boxes have walls. In schools, tests are passed and grades given for memorization and not for understanding. The 4.0 average grade students usually wind up working for the 2.5 grade average students who have had the courage to think outside the box without the restrictions of mere memorization. High grades are largely produced without knowing what Richard Feynman's Father exemplified with his statement to young Richard as *"nothing about the duck"*.

Colleges are set up to learn and do research. They are funded by government or companies desiring a particular outcome for the research that will support their business plans. Institutions of higher learning provided a way for students to engage in various endeavors as they might choose with the guidance of those previously educated by the system but it is important to note that these institutions are for education and research, not for the implementation of new innovations. A box is created by the limitations of the knowledge and the tools used to make determinations in science or the arts.

Innovation and the development of new systems and ideas are far more frequently done by creative and enterprising individuals who take what they learn and apply it individually to change the world around them. They never stop learning. It takes a high level of ingenuity and a driving motivation to step out of the box created by peer pressure and the limitations of a mere college education into a world of individual experimentation and uncertainty. It also takes courage, that courage that says *"I don't particularly care what other people think"* That is not to say you don't care about others but that you have made the determination that you will not be deterred by the opinions of others who don't share the vision that you have. Your peers will laugh, point criticizing fingers and even mock you along the way but you have the courage to let that run off like water on a duck, for you know that if and when you get the job done, they will respect you, even the loudest of mockers.

Anyway, the idea of cleaning air would not leave me alone. It kept coming back as I considered the possible applications. Imagine for a moment what the world would be like if there were no pollution, especially in the air we breathe. People are getting sick all around us and if we are around them, when they cough, sneeze or shake your hand, they expose you to the same sickness that they have. Kids stay home from school a lot for illnesses and they bring the bacteria and/ or viruses they picked up at at school home with them to expose the rest of the family. Dad gets sick and he can't go to work, losing a day's income and a delay in the work agenda on the job, costing the company in lost time. Mom gets sick while burdened with the illness of other family members. Disease is everywhere. The financial losses for all involved are immeasurable, however significant.

Even after applying the best known ventilation, HEPA filtration and UV technologies in hospitals, 30% of surgical site infections are still caused by airborne bacteria. Hospitals are plagued with staphylococcus aureus (staph) infections that they try to avoid responsibility for because they might get sued by patients contracting the disease during a hospital stay. Staph is purported by the hospitals to be caused by bacteria found on the skin of the patients while the fact is that it is notoriously rampant in the nostrils. Ebola the same. It took a long time for the Center for Disease Control (SDC) in the United States to admit that Ebola was in fact transmitted in the aerosols vented by sneezing, coughing or just plain breathing by infected patients. Why, because there was no known way to detect or remove them from ambient air.

The air in homes is rampant with a myriad of airborne particles and gases that are harmful to human health. According to the Environmental Protection Agency, the average home is two to five times more toxic than the outdoor environment. The International Agency for Research on Cancer and the World Health

Organization have concluded that *"80% of all cancers are attributed to environmental rather than genetic factors, including exposure to carcinogenic chemicals, many of which are found in household cleaning products"*. In recent years it is found that people spend as much as 90% of their time indoors, especially in hot summers in the tropics and the winters of the northern and southern hemispheres. While indoors, they are exposed to allergens and toxic air, perhaps contributing to the more frequent incidence of autism. The diseases of potatoes and vegetables have been nearly alleviated by simply eliminating airborne pathogens from storage environments. What would this technology do for human environments? They need to be cleaned up for health's sake.

Ventilation can reduce the population and density of harmful airborne organisms. However with modern day air conditioning in summer and heating in winter months, ventilation is used less and the indoor air is not as frequently replaced by outdoor air. Ventilation cannot completely eradicate indoor pollutants. In fact, in the springtime, allergens are rampant in the outdoor air. In the fall in the northern hemisphere, airborne bacteria and mold spores that have been multiplying all summer are found to be more prevalent in the outdoor air. Ventilation that simply replaces indoor air with outdoor air can bring particles into the atmosphere that are different and that can cause more frequent incidence of allergies, bacterial infections and mold related illnesses.

HEPA filters have been employed in homes, hospitals and offices along with ultraviolet light and electrostatic precipitation (ESP) devices to help keep the air free from harmful airborne particulates. HEPA filters cannot stop the huge majority of viruses. Most viruses are between 5 and 300 nanometers in size. 1,000 nanometers is equal to one micron. HEPA filters will only collect particles as small as 300 nanometers or 0.3 micron. Viruses are too small for HEPA filters to capture, yet viruses are the cause of many of the common diseases experienced by mankind.

Nature does not use filtration to clean the atmosphere. Water is the air cleaning mechanism employed by nature. A technology that could copy the process used by nature to clean the air and apply it to indoor environments would solve the problems of human illness in a big way. I knew I had it but getting it applied was meeting with more and more resistance from established corporations and the universities that were largely funded by these same corporations. Government was not solving the problem because cabinets and the bureaucracies formed by government were being administered by representatives from these huge corporations and by their paid lobbyists that prey upon the ignorance of politicians and win their approval and support by flattery, cronyism and special favors.

In the mean time, people were dying of air pollution. I heard of a mine in West Virginia that caved in and left the miners trapped with no oxygen. The rescuers were drilling a large hole with the intention of bringing the miners out, a slow process. A smaller hole that could have been drilled quicker would have allowed DMV to vacuum contaminated air out and replace it with clean fresh air. I made a call but was ignored because of the panic and frustration of the rescuers trying the ideas of familiar systems without success. It was desperation for them and in the noise of the moment they could not hear me. I did not have the resources to bring my machine to the site and set it up for them. Miners died and I was sad that I could not reach them in time. I longed for the day that DMV could save them and others like them.

Work environments everywhere were, and still are in need of clean air. Hydrogen sulfide (H2S) gas has been silently killing workers around the world. In every city in the world there is a sewage treatment plant and supporting sub stations with vaults that accumulate the poisonous gas produced from raw sewage, creating an environment that is extremely life threatening. H2S gas is heavier than air so it will stay down inside a vault that is accessed by a manhole and will not vent naturally on its own. The gas smells like rotten eggs and is commonly referred to as "rotten egg gas" for that reason. The human olfactory will smell it in small amounts but will become desensitized within 2 to 15 minutes as concentrations increase to a point where it can no longer be detected by smell, a life threatening condition. City employees have descended into manholes and failed to return. When a second man has gone down to the rescue, he has also died, followed by another until it is finally realized that suffocation and death were the reason for their failure to return.

H2S is also a dangerous problem in oil production facilities. It naturally occurs with petroleum related gases that are extracted from deposits beneath the earth's surface. As petroleum is transported, the gas will concentrate in sub-stations and work rooms. In recent years, monitors have been produced for workers to carry with them to detect this dangerous gas in time to remove themselves from the contaminated environment before they are stricken breathless and cannot move. Concentrations of 800 parts per million with kill a human within 5 minutes. Concentrations of 1,000 ppm or more will cause immediate collapse with loss of breathing after inhalation of a single breath.

Scavenger chemicals have been developed to neutralize H2S gas but getting the chemicals to mix readily without a high residence time has been a problem. The residence must occur in a containment vessel or after directly injecting the chemical into a contaminated room. Before I became aware of the development of the scavenger chemicals. I tested a small DMV unit on a sewage lift station in Branson, Missouri attempting to arrest the H2S gas by mixing ozone with the contaminated gases. The test using ozone failed.

Since that time and after developing a revenue source in the potato industry, further work is being done by contract with D&S Automation, an Idaho Company to move forward with the application of DMV for neutralizing H2S gases in various work environments. The problem of too much residence time and inadequate mixing is eliminated by moving the contaminated gases through the DMV simultaneously with a scavenger chemical and recovering it in the DMV separation tank. Finally, this death threatening problem can be fixed and workers' lives can be saved by quickly cleaning the tanks, work rooms and vaults prior to human entry or access for servicing.

The testing that was done at the Rhone Poulenc elemental phosphorous plant at Silver Bow Montana proved a 99.65% capture efficiency of Polonium 210 radio active particles as small as 0.4 micron in a single pass through the DMV. Polonium 210 is the deadly substance that was used to assassinate the Russian spy, Alexander Litvinenko in October 2006. Litvinenko died of induced acute radiation syndrome after three weeks in a British hospital. Author and noted Trump supporter, Roger Stone was poisoned by polonium 210 in late 2016. He had become famous for his outspoken support of Trump and for evidence he had published revealing the illegal activities of certain famous and influential figures in the US Government, including the Clintons. After blood tests conducted by Mt. Sinai Hospital in Miami Beach, Florida, a substance that had the characteristics of polonium 210 was detected in a substantial but not quite lethal amount in the blood of Roger Stone. Polonium 210 was also suspected to have been the substance used to assassinate PLO leader Yassar Arafat.

The use of DMV technology in the home becomes more attractive for stopping the circulation of viruses, allergens and bacteria in the interior of the home than for radio active materials that might be released by terrorists in a community by way of a dirty bomb. However, the added air cleaning capacity along with knowing that a Humigator is operating in a home can give additional peace of mind in the event of such an occurrence. Air within the walls of a home can be kept cleaner than the outside air by applying the principals of natures air cleaning mechanism implemented by a machine that is installed in the mechanical room that circulates and cleans the air. At this writing, the marketing of Humigation is yet to be developed for home and office customers but it is an obvious step that will surely be developed by IHT or by some other innovative and visionary company contracted with IHT in the very near future.

More than 6 million students, representing 14% of the student population missed 15 days or more of school in 2013 -14 in the United States. Students in this category are labeled by the school system as chronic absentees. All 50 states base funding on student population and attendance. Absenteeism is estimated to cost the public schools $ billions each year. Although the total number of absentees in schools is not completely attributed to sickness, sickness plays a huge role in it. Since students get sick by being exposed to other students who are sick, epidemics such as flu can occur because of the spread of the diseases through the air in the schools. Cleaning the air to the extent of removing airborne bacteria, asthma and allergen triggers and mold spores from school environments would increase student health and alertness.

The effective removal of airborne viruses and allergens would decrease absenteeism in schools and work places by a high number. It would also prevent the spread of disease caused by airborne bacteria and viruses in hospitals. Getting the attention of these institutions and convincing them that it can be done is another hurdle caused by tradition and habitual technology barriers. Again the cost of introducing such invasive technology to institutions that are governed by committees and groups of administrators is nearly impossible for a small company. One is always pigeon holed to the point that nothing about the concept of such change moves forward. Tradition has required the support of the research and advocacy of a credible college or university. Funding for such research has only been available through government grants and by the companies that had the capital to sponsor the research. Getting a company with the necessary capital and determination to sponsor such research was in my case, always stopped by the NIH (not invented here) factor and/or a conflict of interest. I found that companies don't buy ideas, they buy companies with established products. Solo inventors don't have much of a chance in such a political climate. There had to be a way to develop the market without the support of colleges or companies with enough capital to do it. I had to find a way to develop DMV on my own.

So, in 2010, after some market research and experience with another company's product, I started a business to develop, sell and distribute my own brand of whole body vibration machines, another invasive technology. I re-designed the product to meet the special requirements of my target market and had the machine built in China according to my specifications. I owned the brand and controlled the product entirely. I imported the machines in shipping containers of 106 machines per container and sold them one by one to customers as I developed the customer list largely by knocking on doors and by word of mouth. The business did not produce a great deal of revenue, mostly because of my diverted attention to my real goal, but it was enough for me to finance and get started placing Humigators with Idaho potato growers at profitable prices. It was a refreshing beginning and a profitable opening in the air purification market. Potatoes were being stored in a cleaner environment than were humans. I hoped to soon be able to address human health needs as well.

It was a lonely place to be, a one man show for four years of constant diligence. I needed help but could interest nobody in helping me. I had to be the scientist, the inventor, the product developer, the manufacturer, the salesman, the servicer, the customer relations manager, the bookkeeper, the banker and everything else that was needed to get this fledgeling started. It was slow and tedious but it worked. Fortunately, after each installation, most customers were happy with the results. The machine I had developed prevented the spread of dreaded fungal diseases caused by pathogens without chemical applications that were being unsuccessfully tried to eradicate them.

Humidity was produced by the machines as residual microscopic droplets that stayed airborne. The tiny, invisible droplets were being produced by the high energy impaction and low pressure zones in the Humigator after capturing the microscopic pathogen particles and encapsulating them into the water in the separation tank. That was a bonus I had not anticipated. It turned out to be a significant bonus because potatoes are sold by weight and keeping the humidity high in the storage area kept the potatoes from shrinking. It was also found that potatoes could be rehydrated, gaining weight and integrity after shrinking in the field before harvest. Healthy potatoes were becoming the norm. Humans would have to wait their turn for a little longer.

CHAPTER THIRTEEN

FREEDOM AND PERSONAL RESPONSIBILITY

IF YOU CAN'T BELIEVE YOUR DOCTOR, WHO CAN YOU BELIEVE?

I will give a physical example in this chapter to illustrate the difference between accepting personal responsibility and giving it away to others. Giving it away to others is a form of slavery by choice. It is a cop out to be used by lazy and ignorant people with a sense of entitlement. There are others who would enthusiastically take it to establish dominion over the people but they really have no authority to take it. Even if they did, they would eventually find that they have taken control of nothing in the long run, for such transference by an individual is a step toward voluntary extinction. Actually it is really impossible to pass personal responsibility to others unless we would rather cease to exist. Let me illustrate with a rather lengthy example of how it works in personal health.

Whole body vibration is an example of an invasive technology that slightly interferes with corporate trends created by big pharmacy companies and the vast, government approved medical related professions, including medical schools and the doctors they educate and produce.

There are countless alternative, free and low cost treatments for medical maladies. However, having no monitoring nor approval from anyone, they are seldom research proven and are always kept in doubt in the eyes of the public. There are exceptions but the exceptions are not easily identifiable. They are not supported by the food and drug administration, nor by any alternative checks and balances system. Regulation is necessary, even in a free society. Alternative preventive medicine is preferable over pharmaceuticals to maintain a healthy lifestyle but in a jungle of alternatives and money making schemes it is hard for each individual to find the proper combination and make the right choices.

Whole Body Vibration technology (WBV) was first developed for Russian Cosmonauts and U.S. Astronauts to restore and preserve muscle and bone mass that was lost during long term stays in zero gravity space. Zero Gravity means no stress on bone and muscle structures. Exercise is essential to sustain bone and muscle mass. Sedentary living, a most common condition of office workers and senior citizens, has a similar effect with outer space because muscle and bone masses, like agency and responsibility, are not challenged enough to preserve their integrity. If you don't use it, you lose it. Complete idleness of muscles eventually results in paralysis because the brain no longer connects to the nerves that activate muscles that are no longer used.

The space research programs stirred an interest in academia and the medical world, mostly in Europe and Asia. Recently, more work has been done in universities across the United States. A number of studies were done in the 1980s and 90s, and were applied to a variety of conditions and applications. If you want to do some research, there are volumes of studies on the internet, most of which show very positive and encouraging results. However, technology that interferes with medical business models that include the marketing of new drugs and the addressing of medical maladies by treatment after the fact is not readily welcomed by medical professionals. Preventive medicine, exercise and healthy living do not call for frequent visits to the pharmacy or the medical professional. Here again, personal responsibility trumps the doctor. You know your own body better than anyone.

I was first introduced to whole body vibration using an oscillating vibration plate with variable frequencies of movement. I noticed right away that I felt warmer and my hands and face were more flushed. This aroused a curiosity in me and motivated me to look into the physics of the blood, arteries, veins and capillaries. Arteries are the big blood vessels, veins the medium sized ones and capillaries the tiny tubes that feed individual cells and organs of the body. I have since tried and done research on vibration plates of different types.

The most common vibration plates are of two types, triplaner and oscillator. The triplaner has two motors, each vibrating in a different direction, both up and down and sideways. The oscillator has only one motor and moves in a teeter totter motion, up on one side while down on the other. After doing the research and my own experimentation, I have come to the conclusion that the triplaner vibration plate is an overkill attempt toward maximum benefit, kind of like overdosing on drugs or vitamins. If one is good for you then two must be better. This impression may also be used to stimulate a higher price and more profit to the manufacturers and distributors. Triplaners are more expensive than oscillators for obvious reasons, they have more moving parts.

Further, It doesn't seem logical, from a physics point of view, that vibration in more than one direction simultaneously is helpful to the body. Oscillation, on the other hand, is a coordinated way of communication with blood and tissue cells of the body, stimulating the fluids and muscle fibers in an action/reaction coordinated manner. The body will respond by reflex to one direction of movement but the reflex response becomes confused if the movements are in more than one direction at a time. Besides, oscillator plates with a single motor are affordable for the average user and are also most beneficial for everyday conditioning.

The body responds to movement or disturbance of balance with a reflex action. This reflex action is involuntary and happens even without a person being aware that it is happening. I had a friend who said that he could always tell if his wallet was in his back pocket because if it wasn't it would cause one side of his butt to fly up higher than the other. I'm not sure his body was that sensitive but I do know that I will tip over if my balance mechanism does not involuntarily correct my center of gravity without my making a conscious effort to remain upright whenever my fulcrum is displaced.

Oscillating vibration plates work better in cooperation with the body's natural responses. The exercise experienced with an oscillation plate stimulates soft tissue, blood and muscle for balanced exercise without effort on the part of the user. First use will make some ordinarily sedentary subjects a little stiff the next day. Gym enthusiasts will tell you that is a good thing. It means the muscle is torn down a bit and is now in the process of developing more mass and becoming stronger than before.

Professional sports teams and some doctors use more sophisticated vibration plates for recovery and conditioning. These units are expensive, running in cost from about $12,000 to $40,000 or more per machine. It is difficult for an average home owner, particularly a retired one, could afford such a machine in the home. Oscillating plates are more beneficial and have become more affordable for the average home owner at about 10% of that cost.

WBV has yet to be recognized by those in control of the medical regulatory regime as an established cure for diseases. The regulatory regime and the law makers in the government are heavily lobbied by the drug producers, and doctors are heavily marketed by the representatives of those drug producers. An invasive technology such as whole body vibration for the treatment of disease cannot and will likely not be accepted into their circles. WBV is not purported to be a cure for diseases. However, it has been shown to be an effective mild exercise for the rehabilitation of the soft tissue surrounding joints after surgery. Patients using WBV after knee surgery have recovered in as little as half the time of patients using ordinary rehabilitation by itself.

Customary exercise such as running, weight lifting, bike riding and even walking target certain bone and muscle groups, leaving others somewhat unchallenged. The muscle used for strenuous activities such as these are mostly the larger muscles of the body. However, there are hundreds of smaller muscles, such as involuntary sphincter muscles, that may remain comparatively unchallenged during strenuous exercise.

According to my research, there are approximately 50 sphincter muscles in the body. Sphincters muscles control the dilation of the eyes and the flow of fluids in the body. Sphincters can be thought of as valves because that is precisely what they are. They are most ordinarily recognized as the muscles that control the flow of food and fluid substances from glands and even the stomach to the small intestine and beyond and also the elimination of waste by ordinary fecal and urinary functions of the body.

Incontinence is caused by a weak sphincter muscle that doesn't have the strength to hold the pressure in the bladder or the large intestine. Coughing and sneezing can apply pressure that exceeds the ability of a low integrity sphincter to hold. Urinary incontinence is a common problem for women whose sphincter muscles have been weakened by pregnancy and child bearing. Sphincter muscles are maintained by exercise, the same as other muscle groups.

Whole Body Vibration does not focus on specific muscle groups the way that conventional exercises do. Instead, it effects all of the muscles simultaneously. Whole Body Vibration stimulates the circulation of blood through the tiny capillaries that provide oxygen and other nutrients to all of the bones and muscles of the entire body.

The body is moved and controlled by both voluntary and involuntary muscles. There is no status quo with muscle fiber. Muscles increase in size and strength with exercise and will weaken and deteriorate where there is none. Pain is the most common deterrent to human determination to exercise. It is discouraging to work through pain, even if we know that it is the only way to get rid of it. In most cases, exercise will alleviate muscle and other soft tissue pain but it takes time and effort. Whole body vibration provides a way to engage the exercise in shorter time and with less effort, making it easier to work through the pain.

Stagnant blood flow allows the settling of suspended particles which may obstruct blood vessels and result in an accumulation of cholesterol or a blood clot, causing a stroke or a heart attack, or the blockage of the tiny blood vessels that deliver oxygen and nutrients to other parts of the body, such as the arms, legs and skeletal muscles. The unobstructed flow of the blood stream is essential to preserving the function and integrity of all of the organs of the body. WBV shakes the body much like a can of paint at the hardware store and it serves a similar purpose, to suspend all particles in the fluid for even distribution.

While considering the elements of the body, a consideration can also be made of their actions and reactions in relationship with one another. One of the most important components of the body is blood but the mechanisms that transfer the blood are just as important. The heart is mostly muscle, a muscle that feeds itself through its own functions. All other muscles are fed by the mechanism of the heart too. The body would have no energy without the muscles of the heart pumping the blood through them and dropping off the fuel that keeps them going along the way.

Blood is a suspension of particles in a fluid called a colloid. The particles can be separated by mechanical centrifuge which is like the force of gravity enhanced by centrifugal motion. Keeping the particles mixed and evenly distributed in the fluid (colloid) helps the fluid to flow evenly and with less restriction through smaller tubes and vessels. Consequently, it makes sense that whole body vibration decreases chances for the accumulation of particles such as fat (cholesterol) in any tubes or channels, including capillaries or blood vessels. Research has shown that capillaries and blood vessels are also dilated and flexibility is increased by WBV.

Blood can be gravitationally separated into solid and liquid parts by a centrifuge, separating the blood cells and platelets from the plasma. Fat cells are also carried and distributed by the blood. Suspending the fat cells in the blood stream tends to prevent the accumulation of cholesterol in stagnant areas of the blood vessels. Stagnant or restricted blood flow contributes to the gravitational separation of suspended particles which may accumulate and obstruct blood flow and result in a buildup of cholesterol or a blood clot, causing the blood pressure to rise which may contribute to a stroke or a heart attack. WBV has the effect of helping to suspend the platelets, blood cells and fat particles in the blood stream. We shake paint for even flow and distribution without clogging. Is the paint more important to us than our bodies?

Type 1 Diabetes is an autoimmune disease that occurs when the body's defense system attacks and destroys its own cells. In Type 1 Diabetes, the immune system destroys the cells that make insulin in the pancreas. Insulin is a hormone that is used by the body to convert sugars and carbohydrates into the energy that is needed for our bodies to maintain normal function. Once these cells are destroyed, the body does not produce enough insulin to convert the sugars and carbohydrates that are consumed. This can lead to other, life threatening illnesses and diseases. Studies have shown that approximately 75% of diabetics die of heart disease, stroke, or other types of circulatory problems brought on by the disease, not by the disease itself.

The pancreas is an endocrine gland. The islets are a compact collection of endocrine cells arranged in clusters and cords and are crisscrossed by a dense network of capillaries. The capillaries of the islets are lined by layers of endocrine cells in direct contact with vessels, and most endocrine cells are in direct contact with blood vessels, by either cytoplasmic processes or by direct apposition. A healthy circulation system is obviously essential for the prevention of the onset or progression of diabetes.

Poor circulation can contribute to the blockage of the tiny blood vessels that deliver oxygen and nutrients to other parts of the body, such as the arms, legs and skeletal muscles. The unobstructed flow of the blood stream is essential to preserving the function and integrity of all of the organs of the body. It also helps circulation to drink a lot of water. Drinking water provides the necessary fluid for the blood stream to carry the essential particles throughout the body and for the heart and blood vessels to do their job efficiently.

Let's talk physics for a moment. All things are made of a combination of basic elements. The elements are indestructible. They always exist, although many environmental idealists would rather that some of them would just go away. They demand that the industrialists make them disappear, however unreasonable as it may seem. Mostly political pressure, I'm sure. The human body is made of elements, a combination of many elements that form substances and materials, fluids, fibers and tissues that make up valves, vessels, bones and muscles.

There is need for user awareness with WBV that should be placed at the front of any exercise program, WBV or otherwise. The body is a physical mechanism that functions much like other physical mechanisms. It requires management like other mechanisms do, and it functions in many ways in the same manner. The body is made up of solids, gases and liquids like every other creature, substance or device found in this environment we call "*nature*". The elements are the building blocks for the creation and existence of everything, whether solid, liquid or gas, organic or inorganic.

When we look at our bodies as physical mechanisms like any other physical mechanism, it is likely that our understanding of its needs can be increased and its integrity improved by physical applications. We have pumps, valves, orifices, sphincters, glands and transfer systems that have been widely duplicated by industry to accomplish many mechanical processes. Moving parts, substances and fluids are not likely to become bound up as with stagnation and dormancy, whether in industrial processes or in the human body.

The human body and its waste elimination system is no different than other physical processes in that it requires material and fluid handling by motive force, voluntary or involuntary in order to function properly. Gases, solids and liquids must be passed effectively through the digestive system or the system shuts down, clogs up or becomes non-functional due to stagnation of the motive force (sphincter muscles) that keeps things moving and shuts them off when necessary.

It is pretty hard to imagine not being able to pass gas when necessary. In fact it is impossible to continue to live without that necessary privilege of eliminating the waste byproducts generated by the ordinary and necessary physical functions of the lymph and digestive systems. The gas passed by the human body is largely carbon dioxide and methane. The smelly part is a minute amount of hydrogen sulfide. As previously stated, hydrogen sulfide is deadly if inhaled in concentrations above 400 ppm. This is not likely to happen in ordinary living or co-mingling with our fellow creatures in an elevator. However, I have heard that at least one person has died when cleaning out a lower level hog pen from the heavier than air concentrations of hydrogen sulfide emitted from the hogs. No concern for the hogs of course.

In the last few decades, industry has moved away from manual jobs such as bucking hay or stacking boards or boxes, replacing active lifestyles with sitting all day in front of a desk or computer. Automation has changed lifestyles into less activity and exercise. Exercise programs, designed for the new industry environment have sprung up and people are exercising in other ways. However, senior citizens are largely ignored by the exercise industry that plays heavily on youthful, hard body appearance. The WWII baby boomers are now retiring, rapidly increasing the senior population in the U.S. I should know for I am one. Most seniors shut down at retirement and many of them become so sedentary that bodily functions become impaired. Whole body vibration is wonderful for senior citizens. It provides a means for essential daily exercise for seniors in the privacy of their own homes.

Drug manufacturers, by persuasion and financial incentives, have become the directors of medical treatment. Their lobbying and marketing have moved the use of drugs into dangerous territory for the patients that are marketing their products to. Companies have become compromised in their research to the point that economic benefits to their corporate needs have long overridden the benefits and well being of their customers. Pain killers such as opioids are addictive substances with many harmful side effects. Blood thinners such as warfarin (coumadin) and blood pressure control medicines are marketed as life saving drugs when in fact they are dangerous killers. Coumadin was originally used to poison rats by causing them to bleed to death.

Big, corporate drug manufacturers have developed enormous profitability by promoting drugs instead of human wellness. According to a report by The Daily Conservative Newsletter, in 2014 the profits of the major drug manufacturers were enormous: Novartis - $47.1 billion, Pfizer - $45.7 billion, Merk - $36 billion, Johnson and Johnson - $32 billion, and GlaxoSmithKline - $29.5 billion. It isn't any wonder that in order for these huge behemoth drug companies to survive, they must develop and sell indescribable amounts of their products to the public through extensive advertising, propaganda, lobbying government officials, creating big incentives for drug representatives and by overwhelming the medical doctors who prescribe them. All for money.

These harmful substances, developed by the drug manufacturing corporations have affected many uninformed patients to the point of addiction and even death. Doctors with little time, having done little or no research on specific drugs on their own, believe what the representatives tell them because the drugs they represent have been approved by the government and besides, the drug representative bought lunch.

So, what is wrong with invasive technologies such as natural health alternatives such as whole body vibration exercise? Well it largely boils down to the fact that WBV, like other preventive health measures, generally interferes with the income stream of the medical profession and they aren't expensive enough to provide corporate revenue. If you feel good at home you're not going to the doctor for anything. Consequently alternative medical practices are opposed by many doctors and so called "*experts*" in the medical world. Your doctor is not likely to recommend, or even approve whole body vibration for your condition because he has not been made familiar with it by corporate big drug manufacturers nor by his medical school. Here again, personal choice and responsibility are essential to a happy life. Freedom and healthy lifestyles demand personal responsibility.

You know your own body better than the doctor does, he or she can only generalize your condition with the conditions of others that he or she is familiar with. The responsibility for personal happiness and well being cannot and should not be turned over to another person regardless of his status or expertise. Personal, informed choice and responsibility are essential for happiness and necessary for the existence of true freedom. The Pollyanna Zone requires a good deal of personal responsibility and discernment. Everyone cannot become expert in everything but for those things that affect a person's life, character and well being, in the long run that person has to be personally responsible, regardless of other's opinions or recommendations, whether expert or not. Trust is in the balance and is lacking. Cynicism sets in and the love and respect for fellow man diminishes.

There are some methods, such as diet and exercise that can be understood on a basic and sensible level without full knowledge. Unfortunately, people in societies around the world have been reduced to only common logic. They are largely on their own with only the basics to rely on; still looking for the elusive Pollyanna Zone where trust and compassion in those around them override the profit motive.

CHAPTER FOURTEEN

FREE ENTERPRISE AND THE CONSTITUTION

THE SPIRIT OF THE LAW AND PUBLIC OPINION

I was refreshed by the constitutional aspects of Dec. 2013 rulings by the Federal court in Utah, dealing with both same sex marriages and plural marriage issues. I looked with favor on both of these rulings only through the eyes of the constitutional law and not from a religious nor a philosophical point of view, although I do have both.

A huge characteristic of the constitutional law, supported heavily by Patrick Henry in the 1700s is the complete separation of church and state. As far as same sex marriage goes, there is no logical foundation for such practice and I don't philosophically support it but I don't think the government has any business trying to regulate personal relationships. Having said all of that, I, for one, will defend to my death a citizens right to choose for themselves. That is what was intended in the drafting of the Constitution and the Bill of Rights of the United States by the founding fathers when they pledged their lives, their fortunes and their sacred honor to the cause of freedom. Governments are necessary to maintain order in any society but they should never be allowed by those they govern to run roughshod over the rights of the people.

It seems difficult for the average citizen to separate philosophical and religious beliefs from the laws of the land. Everyone, by nature wants to incorporate them in daily living. The laws of the land are consequently incorporated with religious beliefs in the minds of most people who would have government assume their personal responsibilities. The complete separation of church and state is essential for the protection of freedom of choice in any culture even if there is no church, only a philosophy.

The history of monogamy begins with the combining of church and state, uniting the Roman government with the Roman Catholic Church. It was first instituted for the preservation of the property of the emperor and the Vatican by preventing the fragmentation of the fortunes of the governors and the nobles associated with that combination. The selfish control of wealth and property would be diluted and lost by sharing and distributions to countless family members so in order for it to be preserved, families had to be limited and wide sharing or distribution of wealth had to be prevented or eliminated.

The opinion of the Federal Court, considering a lawsuit filed by Kody Brown, a man with four wives and a national TV show, was a summary judgement that while preserving the "*spiritual marriage*" portion of the Utah State law, the cohabitation prong was eliminated, allowing for religious unions and contractual cohabitations to be legal and lawful as long as a person does not apply for multiple marriage licenses with the State. Because of traditional church and state incorporated philosophy, tradition and reasonable definition of the Constitutional Law at the beginning of the 20th century, the pressure would probably have still been too great for the Mormon Church to carry on with its very existence had it not done away with the practice of creating spiritual plural marriages.

It would take a great deal of traditionally unavailable charity on the parts of both men and women for plural marriage to be the norm in any society. Because of this prevailing element of modern society, the U.S. Court of Appeals chose not to uphold the opinion of the Federal Court in Utah, citing that formal criminal charges had not been brought by the State of Utah against the Browns as their reason for denying it, thereby dodging a constitutional bullet.

Marriage and personal relationships are really none of the business of any government. They have nothing to gain or lose by laws regulating personal relationships except unrighteous dominion and unenforceable control. Governments are not very good at uniting and preserving families. In fact, the opposite is true. It will be interesting to see how long it will take for complete, orderly freedom of choice to prevail. It is not likely to occur in a society where governments choose to ignore constitutional rights in favor of the enforcement of unjust laws to support the accumulation and preservation of wealth by an elite few.

It is important for Americans to understand the basic functions and duties of the three branches of the constitutional government. The legislative is to make laws, the executive to enforce laws and the judicial to judge laws that are passed by the legislature, using the Constitution and the Bill of Rights as a guideline. This structure was set up by the founding fathers to create a checks and balances system within the federal government that would keep the powers of government from being concentrated in a single branch.

By their very nature, in the history of governments, the enforcement arm (executive branch) tends to take over the powers of the other two and runs roughshod over the citizenry, summarily becoming lawmaker, judge and executioner on the streets (police state). And, as history has proven, with governments it isn't long before executive orders overpower congressional lawmaking and the courts to the point of total control and tyranny.

Hooray for the judicial branch and at least some judges with good sense and thank God for the Constitution! The recent rulings of the lower federal courts that tend to preserve freedom for the people are good rulings, whether or not people or institutions are for or against them for philosophical or religious reasons. It is too bad and also hypocrital that one of the rulings was kept and the other struck down. The Constitution of the United States was drafted by inspired men and adopted to preserve the freedom of citizens to pursue any belief or enterprise they choose and to preclude the state from acting upon or regulating such beliefs.

By the way, it is not important to be concerned about stereotypes such as socialism, communism, capitalism, globalism or any other of the "isms". They all have their good and bad characteristics but they are stereotypes. What is concerning is individual human nature. Individuals in high places naturally tend to exercise unrighteous dominion over those they have been elected or appointed to govern, and there are those who have proclaimed themselves rulers because of their riches and high station in the world.

It would be a much better, richer, happier and safer world if all elected or otherwise appointed officials, whether in science, government or religion, realized that they are to serve, not to dictate. Cronyism, peer pressure and aspiring to the honors of men have unfortunately become the norm in governments and no longer the exception. The natural man is more interested in impressing his superiors and colleagues than he is in performing unselfish service for the benefit of the people he was elected to represent.

Something good happens when we pay the price and the greater the good, the higher and more challenging the price. In order to accomplish a good thing or an improvement, the price must be paid first. Faith always precedes the miracle and diligence precedes the result. Instant gratification is temporary and short lived. It is impossible to grow and improve without exercising faith in your vision first. You can't reach perfection immediately, It is not a bad thing to take the first step and then to take one more step at a time. In the words of Vince Lombardi, *"perfection is not attainable but if we chase perfection, we can catch excellence."* Success in the getting, not in the having gotten. Learn to enjoy the trip. To throw away a small improvement, expecting to have the whole blessing at once, will cause one to fall short of the mark. It is like trying to throw a stone across the mighty Amazon River and expecting it to land on the other side.

When the economy slowed down in the U.S. because of the lack of buying power of the citizenry, it was pumped up by extending more credit to consumers. Credit cards became easier to get, loans were extended to more and more with higher risk for payback until slowly and finally disaster hit. We all see the results of that with the 2008 meltdown in the credit market, mostly over real estate. The wealth of the world has now become concentrated into the hands of less than 1% of the population and those who have it have moved their operations to other countries in order to avoid taxes in the places like the United States and to also avoid liabilities for injuries to their workers and the general population.

If you have the impression that the Federal Reserve Bank is not a private institution, I am here to tell you that you are not seeing the full picture. I appreciate all we have learned but it is time for all people of the U.S. to realize that not only is the Federal Reserve run as a private institution, so also is (or just as well be) the U.S. Federal Government, or at least the Executive Branch. The Executive Branch of the U.S. Government has been largely bought and controlled by the same private group as the Federal Reserve ever since its creation in 1914. Congress passed the Federal Reserve Act in 1913 and the power of the financial system was then delegated to the private bankers who of course promised to execute their responsibilities with integrity, like the fox that promised to watch over the chicken coop. The Federal Reserve is not technically purported to be a private institution but it is run by a Board of Governors with a printing press and lots of fiat money, global interests and world encompassing agendas. The foxes watching the coop are the owners of the world's largest banks and corporations.

Global Research has reported: "*The Four Horsemen of Banking (Bank of America, JP Morgan Chase, Citigroup and Wells Fargo) own the Four Horsemen of Oil (Exxon Mobil, Royal Dutch/Shell, BP and Chevron Texaco); in tandem with Deutsche Bank, BNP, Barclays and other European old money behemoths. But their monopoly over the global economy does not end at the edge of the oil patch. According to company 10K filings to the SEC, the Four Horsemen of Banking are among the top ten stock holders of virtually every Fortune 500 corporation.*"

The European banker, Meyer Amschell Rothschild, the magnifier of the previously developed concept of lending money to countries, mostly to finance wars, said in the 1700s: "*Give me control of a nation's money and I care not who makes its laws*" In operational words, let them think that parties and elections matter, stir the pot, hold their attention and keep the people focused on domestic conflicts between Republicans and Democrats, liberals and conservatives while we in the background quietly control the outcome with wealth and indebtedness. Finance wars for both sides, buy up the media with our wealth, feed them lies and create false flag incidents to hold their attention while we quietly turn up the heat and, step by step, screw down the lid until we finally boil the frog and control the entire world by the "*rule of law*" instead of the rules of personal agency, liberty and freedom.

Woodrow Wilson was not the only U.S. President to give in to money and corporate pressure, selling principles for pottage, popularity and election. The status of beholding to bankers and corporations was brought onto the U.S. by the greed of speculative investors and especially deepened by design when private financiers bailed the U.S. people out of the great depression with an increase of indebtedness to themselves in the form of treasury notes purchased with Federal Reserve fiat, printed money. Franklin Delano Roosevelt's "*new deal*" was subscribed from the macro-economic model speculated by John Maynard Keynes. The "*new deal*" was pulled off by executive order, not by the vote of the people, as also was the elimination of the gold standard by the Nixon Administration. Do you think these presidents were not playing "*pat a cake bakers man*" with the money back then? There was no exercise of income tax in the United States before 1935 and the completion of the "*new deal*". Taxing the incomes if the citizens was a condition of the "*new deal*".

The people of the United States have had little to do or say about the way the government or the economy is run for about a century now. Democracy and the Republic have become only dreams ever since bankers and the super rich began to put forth their own candidates, buy elections and provoke wars in order to create national debt, amass more wealth and have their way with the people in the countries of the world.

If you want to know more about how imperialism works, look closely at the lending activities of the World Bank and the International Monetary Fund (IMF). Struggling countries in South America, Asia and the middle east are typically obligated to pay debts that are impossible for them to pay while the loan proceeds and revenues produced by their infrastructures flow into the coffers of a few super rich robber barons. U.S corporations such as Bechtel have been contracted to create infrastructures and extract metals, oil and other resources from their lands, paid for by the loan proceeds while the people become more and more impoverished. The loan funds may only be transferred from one U.S. bank to another to pay U.S. corporate contractors and the poor people of the now indebted country see very little of it, with the exception of $ millions provided to their corrupt leaders who willingly sold principles for pottage and obligated their citizens to pay the debt.

The wealthy globalists run the world's largest Ponzi scheme, backing debt, public commitments and promissory notes with paper money that they have created with a printing press out of nothing of value except the paper it is printed on. They avoid the laws and taxation that has been put upon the people by them and their colleagues. Greedy capitalists have declared themselves exempt from the constitutional laws of their country and from taxation while infiltrating and supporting government in persecuting and prosecuting those who follow their examples. However, they are finally on a course that will soon implement their own demise. It is truly a house of cards.

Capitalism is not the problem, the abuse of capitalism is. The new world order as pursued by the super rich will not work out as planned. There is too much public awareness and conflict with governments such as Russia, China and those of the Western World. They are all competing to be at the top of the heap. The South American countries are admirably leading the way to liberation from the globalist banks lately, telling the bankers to jump in the ocean along with their free trade and national debt programs, much like Andrew Jackson did in the Bank Wars when he was President of the U.S. In 1832 when he said: "*The many millions which this act proposes to bestow on the stockholders of the existing bank must come directly or indirectly out of the earnings of the American people......*

Many of our rich men have not been content with equal protection and equal benefits, but have besought us to make them richer by act of Congress. It is to be regretted that the rich and powerful too often bend the acts of government to their selfish purposes." Andrew Jackson, July 10, 1832

So, who will fix this mess? Does it make sense for us to expect a remedy from the President and the executive branch of our government, the very lackeys who selfishly implemented the problem? Foxes may have good intentions and even promise change but they still eat chicken and suck eggs. It is past time for the Judicial Branch to have more to say about this stuff in a proper exercise of the checks and balances system that was put in place with the constitution of the of the great United States of America. Taxpayers need to collectively exercise their financial rights in the courts of America instead of succumbing to a national debt to be imposed upon our posterity that is impossible for us or them to repay.

Edward Snowden, now famous for disclosing the huge data mining activities of the U.S. National Security Agency has gone through the process of asking himself the question *"If I don't do this. who will"*?. I admire his courage. He has obviously given a lot of thought and probably prayerful consideration to this issue. I believe he will be triumphant in the end, even if he dies trying. He certainly is an intelligent man, backed by careful consideration and insight, as has been demonstrated quite eloquently in his responses to media interviews. I believe that he, like Martin Luther King and Patrick Henry, is really a patriot.

The super rich are not stricken smart just because they are rich. I don't believe that all globalists have an evil intent. However, as a result of their affluence, they generally underestimate the power of truth and the resilience of common men whose souls cannot be bought and who would rather live free and responsibly than as slaves, no matter the cost. However, the self aggrandizing globalists are smart enough to know that debt can be used as a tool to enslave people and countries. The World Bank and the International Monetary Fund have used that tool effectively around the world for many decades now. Freedom will eventually win but it requires uprightness, courage, commitment and immovable dedication.

Raphael Correa, President of Ecuador, branded as a communist by some self interested globalists, has demonstrated the course that must be taken at some point in time by all countries before this yoke will be removed. After getting a doctorate in economics in a U.S. college, he moved back to Ecuador and was elected President of that small country in 2006. By 2008 he had refused to pay the national debt that he claimed was created by an unlawful dictator before his time, closed down the U.S. military bases in his country and filed a $27 billion law suit against the oil companies that ruined the pristine Amazon basin within Ecuadorian borders. As was customary, he was branded a socialist by the imperialists.

No matter where you live in the world, if all of this scares you, don't let it. Some real patriots around the world, including many in the military and police forces, will pledge lives, fortunes and sacred honor to join with and protect you, just as was done in the beginning of great, free countries in the past. Fear is not a useful tool of the free and you have nothing to fear if you are standing where you should. The lines are being drawn more vividly than ever before. The people are now waking up and becoming aware of these atrocities in huge numbers.

The world financial system with its central banks will finally disintegrate. Money is certainly not everything, in fact it has very little value when it is compared to the worth of a man. Humanity will ultimately prevail but not under the iron fist of a handful of rich task masters. Once again the price will be paid for the retention of freedom and the constitution of the United States of America, whatever the cost. Free people on the side of freedom and personal responsibility will win the push and shove contest. Truth will always prevail in the long run. Individuals would do well at any point in time to live within their means and avoid debt, the tool of the enslaver's trade, stay alert and awake, choose which side to serve and stand firmly with your choices.

The U.S. National debt has inflated to $20 trillion and increasing at the rate of $3.87 billion per day. Who obligated the American people to the national debt? Was it the elected representatives of our states or was it done by executive order, by presidents, either Republican or Democrat, whose elections were largely manipulated and supported by those to whom the debt is owed? Many questions loom on the minds of the American people as more and more evidence is revealed in the wake of the 9/11 World Trade Center destruction and the 2008 financial meltdown.

What has created the U.S. national debt and the acceleration of it? To whom is the debt owed and what for? Is it accelerating because of a perceived need to bail out the banks and huge corporations that are backed by the printing presses of the Federal Reserve. These are those whom are intimately connected with the World Bank and the International Monetary Fund. Aren't these the very people to whom a large portion of the debt is owed, created by their onerous and selfish declarations? In his rejection of a bill to reinstate the charter of the Bank of the United States (central bank), Andrew Jackson observed in 1832 "*It appears that more than a fourth part of the stock (of the central bank) is held by foreigners and the residue is held by a few hundred of our own citizens, chiefly of the richest class.*"

Thomas Jefferson warned us not to let the powers of government become concentrated in the executive branch, if we do, we will have tyranny. Is tyranny what we have now? Is the time coming when the

American people will follow the example of Ecuador and declare the national debt to be illegitimate as it clearly was not authorized by the people nor by their elected congressional representatives? Other countries are now taking a hard look at that option.

The problem is not capitalism, it is the abuse of capitalism. There are those, but a few corrupt individuals, sometimes referred to by alternative news media as *"globalists"* or labeled by John Perkins, the *"corporatocracy"* who have used national debt as a tool to exploit a great number of countries around the world, including Iran, Guatemala, Correa's Ecuador and others with the goal in mind to take control of these nations' resources and their people. Wherever this brand of imperialism has been implemented it has plunged the people into poverty and lined the pockets of a few corrupt individuals who are focused only on their own power and fortunes, and who care little about the starvation and enslavement of others. The wealth of the nation and the world has flowed into the hands of a few *"elite"* individuals who now are making moves to use it to take over the world.

When will the American people be ready to take a firm and organized stand against such exploitation. I think it is coming and the trend toward such a stance is accelerating at about the same rate as the national debt. If you are an American citizen, man, woman or child, with or without a job, they would now have you believe that on March 19, 2013, you were individually obligated to pay to their paper economy an amount in excess of $53,000. Where will the money come from? It is impossible to pay such an enormous amount of money, or even the interest on the loan. Something different has to happen. Change is in the wind, and very soon.

By buying into the globalist design to establish absolute power over all people, Barack Obama, the 44th President of the United States, betrayed most of the people who elected him. He became a modern day Judas to even his own race by destroying the respect for Martin Luther King, by undoing civil rights and black equality by executive order and not the will of the people. Millions of white people also mistakenly voted for him simply because he was black to demonstrate that race prejudice was a thing of the past in a free country, that all men should be treated with respect, as it should have been before the civil rights movement.

When Obama was elected Jesse Jackson wept. Why did he weep? Was it because he thought Obama would be a great president or because he was a black man? Quite clearly it was the latter but that should be qualified further by his personal hope and expectation that Obama would represent the freedom of all men. Did the millions of blacks in the U.S. vote for Obama because they thought he would be a great president, a protector of freedom or was it because he was black and they surmised that he would represent their selfish cause against the tyrannical whites? If the latter, voting was the very act of racism in itself. So who are the real racists in the U.S.? Are they black or are they white? Does it really make any difference as far as the principal of freedom is concerned? Of course not. Obama was a traitor to his own race.

When Hillary Clinton failed to be elected President of the United States countless women wept. Why did they weep? Was it because they believed that Clinton would be the best of the two candidates for President of the U.S., or was it because their dreams of having a women elected as President would be so awesome, no matter who the woman was? Did they know who Hillary Clinton really was or did it even matter to them? My, how people are so easily misled by an appeal to their special interest heartstrings. No specific finger was pointing at blacks or women, it was only a figment. This appeared to be the case for just about everyone until recently as awareness is increasing exponentially, mostly via the alternative communication of a free internet.

While you think about that let me put forth another factor that does not divide blacks from whites but on the contrary it pulls them together for a common cause. No good American can ignore the fact that the reason they have enjoyed citizenship in the U.S. is because the Constitution of the U.S. that was intended to provide equal protection under the law and is based on the principal that *"all men (and women) are created equal"*. Thomas Jefferson first declared it in the Declaration of Independence, demanding independence from the tyranny of the English Empire. This principal, as supported by the subsequent establishment of the Constitution of the United States, provided the premise for religious freedom and racial and sexual equality in America.

If you are a Christian, it becomes logical that the very purpose for the creation of the earth and the population thereof would be thwarted if freedom and the agency of man to choose for himself were destroyed or taken away by earthly principalities and powers. If the agency of man is lost there would be no more purpose for the earth or the men and women in it. They would no longer have the capacity to progress or to establish self control or responsibility. A man cannot grow without the freedom to succeed or the opportunity to fail as he chooses for himself.

Obama will go down in history as being the great American Judas, having given away as much of the freedom of the people of any color, gender or sexual orientation as he possibly could during his tenure as the elected President of a free country. He is a dupe, just as Judas was, believing that the powers that be must be served ahead of the freedom and agency of men. The idea that men would be better off if they had no responsibility for their own behavior, that it is better that government take full control of them, destroys the very purpose of living for both the governors and the governed.

Perhaps Obama's pride convinced him that he could become America's first emperor, or even king of the world. Trump, although championed by the free, is in danger of succumbing to the same syndrome. Power, by nature, corrupts. It can be a terrible temptation. The elites will betray one another in the end. Their hollow purpose cannot stand. There is no honor among thieves. They will become the real slaves, slaves to their own agency destroying devices. The whole plan for selfish dominion will implode and turn against them.

Men become free, not by dominion but by service to one another. I have often tried to imagine what life would be like in a world where all things were shared willingly and generously with everyone else. The fact is that there are plenty of resources to support the population of the world and more if they were distributed freely and properly instead of for monetary profit and gain. It is probable that everyone would be rich, having all that they need for a happy and prosperous life. Everything is shared in the Pollyanna Zone and everyone is trusted, unselfish and dependable.

Money and riches have never made a man happy. Dominion over others has never satisfied those who have taken it. Henry Kissinger said that *"power is the ultimate aphrodisiac"*. There may be temporary gratification in having dominion over others but the responsibility eventually becomes too heavy to bear. Then it will crumble under its own weight and those who have usurped it will soon wish to eliminate a great number of those persons they have dominion over. Hence wars and population reduction become more appealing, especially if they contribute to the already overflowing riches of the perpetrators.

It amazes me that these kinds of self exalted people can be fooled into thinking they are somehow elevated above those they have declared dominion over. Do they really think they can take their riches and dominion with them when they die? How can they think they are free when in fact they are slaves to their own selfish devices and the ones over whom they have had dominion are the really free ones. Sure the oppressed have endured many hardships, largely placed upon them by the principalities and powers created by the power hungry masters but in the end, they are free because they have been unselfishly helping their neighbors who have also been under the oppression of the slave masters. In fact, the greater the hardship, the more they pull together. The more they pull together to help one another the stronger they become, the happier they are and true freedom flourishes. The gladiators were stronger and better conditioned than their slave masters.

CHAPTER FIFTEEN

SCIENCE, DISCOVERY AND RESPONSIBILITY

THE ROAD TO TRUTH IS RIDDLED WITH PITFALLS AND DECEPTION

1991 called for additional research. While in Utah in 1984, I had met a brilliant man named John A. Peterson. John was working with a company in Salt Lake City that was developing wireline technology and building wireline trucks for use in oil well logging operations. While with that company John was granted a U.S. patent on a device that the company used for the operation of the wirelines. His previous and continuous work and experience included a time in the employ of Thiokol Corporation, a U.S. Government contractor that played a large part in the development and testing of solid rocket fuel used by NASA in the space program. Among his many achievements he had acquired a patent for a particular control component of the space shuttle fuel. He had also been published in the journal of the American Institute of Aeronautics and Astronautics (AIAA Journal).

Our meeting had been fascinating. It was the beginning of a relationship that would contribute greatly to understanding the chemical aspects of the DMV air scrubber that I had been working on. John was a chemist and he understood the reactionary relationship of the elements under defined conditions to a high degree. He was also very creative and analytical. Unlike so many others, he immediately caught the vision of my theories and after seeing the data produced at the Rhone Poulenc tests, he became eagerly and actively involved with me in further development efforts of the DMV scrubber. We had several conversations by telephone and then one day he brought a Thiokol engineer friend with him from Utah to my shop in Post Falls, Idaho and the three of us spent a couple of days in intense study of the functionality and chemical reaction aspects of my invention.

John was a very bold and confident researcher. Not being availed to electronic tablets in those days, he would work the various ideas and equations out on paper and whenever the idea would come to a change, he would wad the paper and toss it away on the floor. It was not unusual to find as many as 12 to 20 wadded papers around his chair after these sessions. We discussed the aspects and concentrated on finding solutions for the capture of the various chemical combinations produced by the scrubbing of different industrial emissions. Whenever I or his companion engineer would present a problem, John would say, *"We can figure it out right now, in our heads"*. At one time in our discussions, Knowing that NOx was particularly hard to capture, I asked John if he thought we could get NOx with the DMV. His reply was, *"Yes, if we bang it around enough"*. What he was saying was that we could figure out a way if we banged it around *"in our heads"* long enough. At a particularly high point in our studies in that session John said, *"One thing about it, someday, somebody may tie this process but nobody will ever beat it"*. Even today, I still believe he was right.

After a couple of intense days of studying the process, Peterson and his friend got back in John's Audi and drove back to Utah. When they had gone, my confidence had been magnified. A couple of months later, John arranged a slipstream test of the scrubber at a Geneva Steel plant in Provo, Utah. The plant was a major contributor to the air pollution in the Utah Valley around Provo at the time. Geneva had agreed to pay us $5,000 to cover the costs of the test so I loaded the prototype on a trailer in Post Falls, Idaho, and drove it to Utah. I picked up John in Brigham City and we made the appointment to do a slipstream test at the Provo plant. As we waited for an approval of the location of the slipstream and the signal to attach the system, we were confused. After some time, the project engineer responded with a check for the $5,000 and asked us to leave without testing. The plant was soon shut down and abandoned. Another one bites the dust; the third plant to give up continued operations to avoid the Federal Government EPA and their regulations. To say the least, we were again highly disappointed.

John Peterson was also an accomplished classical guitar player. It was a pleasure to sit and listen to his renditions. It was interesting to find that he could not play by ear but he could play even the most complicated of written guitar music. That was exactly the opposite of my guitar technique which was, and still is, strictly by ear. By the spring of 1993, my correspondence with John had waned. His attitude was evidently changing and I began to notice his reduction in enthusiasm. Except for a couple of visits to his home in Brigham City, we didn't see one another much. I didn't know and he never told me that he was suffering from intense headaches. He was fighting a tumor on his brain that could not be satisfactorily removed and he finally died in August of 1995. It was a terrible loss for me and for the effort. John was a great friend and he had a brilliant and humble mind; a magnificent pleasure to work with.

At the risk of sounding intolerably religious, I offer the following observations that I have made throughout my research and strain to find the way things need to be done. In my quest for the truth I have done a lot of praying. I was taught to pray for wisdom by James 1:5 of the Bible's New Testament and have exercised that privilege throughout my life since that time. Following that instruction has opened my mind not only to the possibilities but to the answers that I sought. Science has to be true and correct or, in the alternative, pride, greed or deception leads to superficial, hollow and empty results. One must be honest with himself at all costs, he must be humble and teachable in order to find the truth in science and religion.

The Nobel Prize winner, Richard Feynman told a fascinating story of an experience he had as a small boy while walking with his Father by a pond. He exclaimed to his father, *"look Daddy, a duck"*. His father wisely explained to the boy, Richard that it was indeed a duck and that he could know what it was in every language in the world but he still would know nothing about the duck. With that foundation in his mind, Richard developed one of the most analytical minds of the century. His understanding of physics and the way things work have influenced my thinking and research. Understanding fire and water is really at the heart of all challenges and solutions relating to energy and the environment in the universe. Richard Feynman understood these factors better than others and he explained them in simple terms.

Quantum Mechanics is a popular attempt by students of science to define the universe using mortal mathematics. To describe the universe by such devices produces the same non conclusive result as defining the circumference of a circle by the same method. It is interesting how God answers serious and earnest inquiry with the truth or, in the alternative, he will leave man to his own devices if the man thinks he is smart enough to figure it out on his own. Quantum mechanics finds its origin in chaos because it runs out of options. The limitation of mathematics to measure round things by square approximations also limits precise measurement of many aspects of the universe. Einstein's response to Neils Bohr, Quantum's biggest proponent of his time, *"God doesn't throw dice"*.

"The significance of Einstein's work is that it was really fundamental to an understanding of the nature of the universe, the nature of the world in which we live, and it was characterized by an astonishing amount of originality. New ideas were a part of Einstein's theories. He asked himself the question, at the age of 15, 'If I were speeding along on a motorcycle at the speed of light, what would the world look like? What would I see?' He answered that question 9 or 10 years later in his theory of relativity" Linus Pauling

The American prophet, Joseph Smith, founder of the Church of Jesus Christ of Latter Day Saints, was an innovator. His quest for the truth extended far beyond traditional religion. Whether he is to be believed or not, one must admit that he was a very bold innovator. There can be no doubt that he sincerely sought the truth. When one reads his true (not white washed) history, his character and honesty is evident in his determination, dedication and unselfish service to others. Whether or not he found the truth in all of his work, I leave to the discernment of the reader. What is interesting though is that Joseph Smith and Albert Einstein had at least one thing in common, both viewing the universe, elements, time and space the same way. They both believed that truth could be found by revelation from the source of all truth and that to be inspired was to be enlightened. No new idea has ever been developed by anything less than a revelation of the truth.

At the tender age of 14, a young and inexperienced Joseph Smith, not yet opinionated by a traditional world and having read the Bible's New Testament, followed the instruction in the Book of James and sought his answers directly from the foremost authority, God himself. I don't know if Einstein read the Bible like Joseph Smith did but, much like the American prophet, there is clear evidence that he chose the path to information that was from the source and not from mere mortal speculation. Joseph Smith sought the truth. He wanted to know who he was, why he was where he was, and where he ought to go from where he stood at the time. Seeking these answers, his quest at the time, although motivated by conflicts in the religious doctrines of his day, did not really have much to do with religion. He simply wanted to know the truth.

Einstein did his research in much the same manner. His conclusions on relativity, and they were conclusions, not theory to him, were drawn from an enlargement of his view of the universe, drawn through a process of pondering, humble open-mindedness and pure reasoning, relying more on common sense than on the common, limited devices and mathematical languages of mortal man. Although it is not evident that he perceived it as such, what he had discovered in relativity was really the first course in the definition and means for endless time, immortality and eternal life. After this realization came to him he said he experienced three days of incredible joy and he challenged all who were curious that they would wind up with the same conclusion if they sought it by truthful and sincere means.

Albert Einstein, *"a scientist who believed in God. He worked like an artist more than a scientist, arriving at a theory, not so much by experimental deduction but confidently by intuition. With quantum physics main proponent, Niels Bohr, Einstein had a 20 year argument. He stubbornly held to his own beliefs. He was as though he had a special pipeline to God, saying 'God doesn't play dice' that somewhere his notion of simplicity was the one that was going to prevail."* Abraham, Pais, Einstein Colleague.

Einstein was right and he confidently knew he was right. What was defined by relativity was that time and space are boundless and eternal. Actually, one may even think of them as non-existent since they have no limitations. This concept provides a limitless potential for the growth of men and gods to continually progress in power and understanding. This is how Joseph Smith came to the conclusion by reasoning and revelation that *"As man is, God once was and as God is, man may become"*. He also determined by revelation and not by empirical experience and then disclosed to the world that the elements are eternal. How did he, being uneducated in science, know that if not by revelation?

Einstein later declared that energy and matter are interchangeable. Matter always exists in one form or another. Was relativity the be all and the end all, explaining everything having to do with time and space, of course not but it was a beginning, a course in universal laws and principals upon which to begin the building of an understanding that reaches far beyond the comprehension of mortal man. It did not find its origin in chaos as did quantum mechanics. In the words of Richard Feynman, another Nobel Prize winner. *"I think I can safely say that nobody understands quantum mechanics."*

Time and space have no substance nor definition. What does exist are action and reaction; particles, whether the size of atoms or the size of planets moving about in endless space, microscopically seen dodging one another (Brownian motion) to maintain integrity of substances, sharing of electrons or maintaining a precisely controlled proximity to one another such as planets in relationship with the sun; or large particles flying apart when acted upon by the forces of energy such as propulsion, angular momentum, electromagnetism or gravity. In other words, time and space are endless and immeasurable. Particles and substances (matter) are controlled by forces that are yet to be understood by mortal man and for now are only investigated. Nonetheless they are controlled and organized by some substantial and intelligent someone, operating intelligently and logically somewhere in endless space. This is how Joseph Smith perceived the universe. Interesting that he, like Einstein, perceived it by revelation, logic and intuition, not just by calculations or experimental devices.

"As I grow older the identification with the here and now is slowly lost. One feels dissolved and merged into nature. It makes me feel happy. The greatest experience we can have is the mysterious". Albert Einstein

Engaged in a conversation with Einstein one evening, Linus Pauling made it a point to memorize and record in his own diary what he had said, *"I made one mistake in my life when I signed that letter to President Roosevelt advocating that the atomic bomb should be built. But, perhaps I can be forgiven for that because we all felt that there was a high probability that the Germans were working on this problem and they might succeed and use the atomic bomb to become the master race".* Albert Einstein

It is evident that Einstein perceived God largely in secret since it was not popular to combine science and religion, but he did perceive a God. Were it not so, why would he feel the need for forgiveness, from whom did he expect it would come, and when?

"The scientist (Einstein) comes at the end of his inquiry against a stone wall, against a mystery that transcends understanding. He stands in reverence before the spectacle of nature, with its order, with its system, with its coherence and must reach the conclusion that there is some directing, controlling power which prevents this planet from being smashed into fragments. He even makes the statement to the effect that the religious idea is not one that he can dismiss because he himself has found that there is a realm beyond which human understanding stands impotent and helpless" Abba Eban, Former Foreign Minister and Israeli Ambassador to the United Nations

"His lack of fear of time, his lack of concern of 'how long will it take before I reach my goal?' That, I think in itself translates itself ultimately into a lack of fear of death." Abraham Pais, Einstein Colleague

I might add to Pais' quote that although he did not outwardly share his innermost convictions, Einstein also understood that there was no end to time and that there was not time enough in his brief mortal life to accomplish all that he would like to do. However, he also understood that it did not matter so much that he was unable to finish a study, such as to understand gravity, or any particular project before he died because he thought that he would probably be able to carry on in immortality anyway. The only thing to be lost was mortal man's acceptance and use of the things he had discovered. This gave him an extraordinary abundance of patience, relieved a lot of stress and allowed him time to think and ponder his studies in greater depth. *"Our situation on this earth seems strange. Everyone of us appears here involuntarily and uninvited for a short stay without knowing why. Seeing it is enough to wonder at the secrets".* Albert Einstein

One must stand in awe of the great scientist, Einstein, who was a realist in his thinking, not willing to place his confidence in mere happenstance or even totally in his calculations. All truth demands logic and reasoning. Both Joseph Smith and Albert Einstein understood that well enough to draw their conclusions directly from some real source, where more was known about the things they sought than any mortal man. When questions arose that seemed imperative to causes or declarations, the truth was essential in both of their minds. Neither of them wanted to get caught misleading themselves, nor humanity in a perilous direction. The course had to be true or the destination would be an empty abyss, false and deceptive.

Did they err in the process, of course they did, as all mortal men do. No man is perfect in his understanding but perfection and the success they sought was in the getting, not in the having gotten. The journey to pure understanding of all things is far beyond human comprehension and is indicative of the probability of eternal and endless progression. The trick is staying on the right track, navigating and avoiding the many pitfalls and diversions.

It has been viewed as out of the question by both Smith and Einstein to lie to humanity or mislead them over a precipice guided by falsehood and deception. To do so would lead to their own destruction, in the exact opposite direction they intended for it to go. They both relied upon a higher, more intelligent source for guidance and advice, the source of all science and all truth, the higher power of whomever was coordinating the universe and all things in it, even God, the great organizer of the universe. With the utmost integrity and determination they wanted to lead in the correct direction, precisely as required to achieve the desired, upward, right and proper goal and conclusion. Such determination seems fair to all mankind, reasonable, righteous and imperative.

Joseph Smith said in his now famous discourse at the funeral of King Follett: *"I take my ring from my finger and liken it unto the mind of man, the immortal spirit, because it has no beginning. Suppose I cut it in two; as the Lord lives, because it has a beginning, it would have an end. All the fools and learned and wise men from the beginning of creation who say that man had a beginning prove that he must have an end. If that were so, the doctrine of annihilation would be true. But if I am right, I might with boldness proclaim from the housetops that God never did have power to create the spirit of man at all. God himself could not create himself. Intelligence exists upon a self-existent principle; it is a spirit from age to age, and there is no creation about it. Moreover, all the spirits that God ever sent into the world are susceptible to enlargement. The first principles of man are self-existent with God. God found himself in the midst of spirits and glory, and because he was greater, he saw proper to institute laws whereby the rest could have the privilege of advancing like himself--* " Joseph Smith Jr.

George S. Patton Jr. once wrote in his diary *"Perhaps I would not be satisfied unless I was God, and somebody probably outranks him"*. It may or may not have been a flippant remark but the declaration was illustrative of man's eternal progression. Even God is still progressing. Joseph Smith would have agreed and I believe Einstein would as well. I certainly do. Onward and upward forever, there is great adventure ahead. I look forward to it with enormous enthusiasm.

CHAPTER SIXTEEN

THE TRANSITION

WINNING REQUIRES COURAGE AND COOPERATION

Consider what would happen to the economy if petroleum and nuclear energy were to be replaced by clean water hydrogen. Besides the fact that the oil companies would go out of business, about 10 million jobs related to the petroleum industry would be lost world wide. This represents less than 5% of all of the jobs in the world. Nuclear energy would also become obsolete. There are estimated to be a little over 100,000 jobs related to nuclear energy in the United States, serving 99 nuclear reactors generating about 20% of the electricity used. Coal powered plants generate about 33%, natural gas, 33% and hydropower represents only 6%. Alternatives such as wind, solar, geothermal and other renewables, just over 7%. The replacement of all of these industries at the same time, which is highly unlikely, would represent less than 10% of the total world economy. The jobs created by a water energy economy would be considerably fewer than traditional methods but an estimate of 5 million jobs would only displace workers worldwide by about 3%. Not really a huge impact on the world economy

The automobile industry would not be negatively impacted by an alternative fuel, except for the changes necessary to adapt engines to burn water. In fact, there would probably be more demand for cars and trucks if there was not so much drain on the budgets of car owners for purchasing fuel. What would require the most attention would probably be the infrastructure to accommodate more traffic on the roads and bridges. This would only create more jobs to replace those lost in support of petroleum and atomic energy. The petroleum industry would not be entirely obsolete because petroleum is used for the production of many products not related to fuel. Plastics, asphalt, lubricants and other products are also produced from petroleum. According to the Bureau of Labor Statistics, the average family in the United States spends 1/3 of their budgets on fuel. The fact is that the economy will grow and become very robust when consumers are able to apply more of their budgets to spendable income and not so much on fuel for energy.

Before the Pollyanna Zone, there has to be a step by step process toward a complete change. Since pollution has become the norm and petroleum and coal have grown to be the deep tradition that they have, it needs to be addressed, one source at a time, even in the face of monstrous resistance. As long as the corporate/government establishment is run by a few powerful people that are controlling policies, jobs, making money and depending on the industries that pollute to feed their business models and political favorites, they will continue to provide a powerful resistance to innovative technologies that cost a fraction of their methods and invade their special interests. The potato storage application of humigation is a very small, yet significant start, but it has become an incomparable process and can no longer be ignored. It is a nice foot in the door for those of us who seek to clean up the planet and do what we can to provide freedom and clean living for the people who inhabit it. Knowing that it can be easily done and not being able to do it has been frustrating to say the least but, on the positive side, it has brought to the fore an understanding of the world as it really is. To just get a foot in the door is a big, necessary step to defeat the resistance but such a movement also requires public and consumer support.

Consumer interest for the introduction of new technology is hindered by tradition and loyalty to products and service companies that they have depended on for years to provide support for their respective industries. Sometimes, for a new method to emerge, an old one has to become troublesome or economically unreasonable. Filters are troublesome in that they gradually plug and periodically need to be changed and disposed of. Hazardous gases such as hydrogen sulfide, sulfur dioxide and oxidized nitrogen have not been sufficiently scrubbed or kept from the atmosphere by any method. Harmful particulates such as lead, mercury and other heavy metals are being discharged into the air because an effective way to stop it has been lacking. Before a total elimination of these harmful emissions can occur, the industries that produce them need to be replaced with cleaner energy and the reduction or elimination of the use of most chemicals. The use of chemicals for beneficial purposes such as pesticides. herbicides and disinfectants has its damaging affect as well. It is a two edged sword. Like the drugs that have been developed for human use, there are harmful side effects that are harmful to the environment and to the human race.

A transition from atomic energy and petroleum to water energy would only upset a few very powerful people, the very people who control and dictate, not only economic interests in their favor but also the economy itself. Whether or not a transition can be made by replacing traditional technologies with clean, new ones, the old ones will eventually fail of their own doing. Lies and deceptive practices cannot prevail in the long run. The integrity of individuals pursuing such tactics will be undermined by lack of trust among themselves. Cronyism, supported by deception will be found out by those being deceived and sale of their their wares will dwindle until their business models will die for lack of customer support. A house built on a sandy foundation will not stand when a storm comes and the bigger the house, the more pressure on the foundation until it finally crumbles of its own weight and its porous integrity.

All of these deceptive and imperialistic practices must go away before peace and prosperity of the people of the world can be enjoyed, and they will. Public awareness has been magnified by internet alternative news sources that deal in truth instead of the slanted news and propaganda put forth by the corporate owned, mainstream news media. Countless internet news sites have been formed and discovered in the last decade. Alex Jones and Infowars, although quite radical at times, have been and still are the 20 year experienced spearhead of the movement. Alex Jones has introduced many other truth seeking internet broadcasters to the public by interviews and they too are expanding their influence through their rapidly growing number of viewers. Radio hosts like Michael Savage and even Rush Limbaugh have increased the number of truth seekers. The movement has created an avalanche of public awareness as the information becomes correctly seen and better understood.

The internet has also been used of course to put forth some false or *"fake"* news, causing some true internet news sources to come into question by the public on certain points and making some of the information confusing and hard to accept or understand. However, backup, support information and the testimonies of the many whistle blowers that have come forth are canceling the false news reports because of the free wheeling internet and the freedom of communication it provides. Public awareness will quickly create the opposition necessary for the disintegration of prevalent lies and deception. The corporations that are owned and the governments that have been controlled by the few who would prefer to be self appointed rulers and slave masters over a free people are rapidly disintegrating for lack of public support. The Pollyanna Zone is just around the corner, people worldwide would be well advised to get qualified and be prepared for it.

CHAPTER SEVENTEEN

ENTERING THE ZONE

FREEDOM IS REAL, NOT IDEALISTIC

From this point on, dear reader, you are going to have to let your mind accelerate into imagination and a consideration of the possibilities. We now know that water can replace fossil fuels and atomic energy sources. As we imagine what the world would be like with water for energy, a true water world, one has to elevate to a higher standard of living. Corruption and pollution, both moral and industrial must be set aside and abandoned. The industrial pollution of the earth has expanded exponentially and simultaneously with the corruption of human behavior. There are only two ways for a man to go, up or down. One direction is creative, the other destructive. Daily, even momentary choices of one or the other are made every day by each individual.

An attitude of self destruction, although the possessor of such an attitude may not be aware of it, is at the heart of moral deterioration. When a man has no confidence nor self esteem conducive to his own initiative and improvement, he deteriorates. There is no status quo. Stagnation deteriorates all objects and aspects in nature. Neglect and laziness will pollute and eventually destroy any endeavor to improve circumstances. An attitude of entitlement or instant and temporary gratification in any individual places demands on hollow and empty sources that are actually non-existent. Value demands production and requires the ambition of someone willing to produce it. One cannot grow without working and without working no individual can enjoy the fruits of his labor. If anything is free, it quickly vaporizes and cannot be appreciated. The reward is personal growth. Growth is in the getting, not in the having gotten.

With that background in place, let your imagination soar to the greater heights of a world without pollution, where energy is free. Can it be done? Of course it can. It has been proven that it can be done, both morally and scientifically. The only obstacle is human nature and the greed, power and hollow gratification of a few individuals that must be moved out of their places in order for it to happen. Am I talking revolution here? No, a war is not necessary. Moral deterioration occurs naturally. Greed and power are destructive characteristics and subscribers to such will naturally deteriorate into oblivion. A house built on the sandy soil of deception, corruption and lies will eventually cave in and destroy itself. It will not be a pretty sight for those whom have become dependent on that house of cards and the transition will be painful for a lot of people for a time. However, when that finally happens, the pollution that is a natural characteristic of such attitudes will go away. Replacing it is easy and quick. There are those of us who know how to do it and hopefully this book will help our numbers to increase. We are ready for the change and the transition to clean energy and environment can happen overnight. Like good boy scouts, stay morally clean and be prepared, for a change is coming soon.

Water is the friendliest, most plentiful and versatile substance on earth. It makes up a large portion of the bodies of everything that is alive. Everyone knows that it will put out fires but not everyone knows that it can also create them. Not everyone knows that water is the mechanism of naturally clean air in the atmosphere. It is not a matter of harnessing water, it is a matter of applying it, cooperating and coordinating with it. With respect to growth, movement, even life itself, especially long life, water is our best friend, anywhere on the planet. Without water there would be no life. Energy exclusively produced from water will immediately clean up the atmosphere in the millennial Pollyanna Zone. There is no need for industrial emissions control equipment, including scrubbers that use water for cleaning the air emitted from industrial smoke stacks and internal combustion engines. Water may still be used for controlling the spread of harmful viruses, bacteria and mold spores through the atmosphere of occupied spaces but the power to run the machines are now generated from the combustion of hydrogen and oxygen in water.

Imagine, a new, energy efficient power plant has been built just down the road from your house. It is made up of a conversion of internal combustion engines that have been converted from burning natural gas to burning water. The water is being recovered after combustion and reused to produce more energy and electricity. The air emitted from the plant is clean and free of particulates and harmful gases. Electricity is less than half the price that it used to be. The public power grid is backed up at your house by an internal combustion generator that you are fueling with your garden hose. You fill the tank on your car and truck with the garden hose as well.

When you awake in the morning after breathing the clean air that is dust, bacteria, mold, radiation and virus free throughout the night, your senses are sharpened, your head is clear and your energy level is at its peak. Your enthusiasm for the activities ahead of you has been increased by a good night's rest. Your ambition is no longer impaired by harmful and impure substances taken into your lungs and into your blood stream. Your thoughts are conducive to progress and accomplishment, not to giving in to a sick and destructive feeling, impaired and fueled by the previous lies and deception, and the pollution and destruction that used to be all around you. You can see forever. The air is clean. No more airborne chemicals to make you sick and slowly destroy your body. No more cancer nor radiation sickness. You are now free to go forward at a faster pace, to grow and to increase and you feel equal to the challenges and up for doing whatever it takes to engage in the progress.

Your neighbor is in the same zone, happy and enthusiastic, eager to cooperate, to help, to engage and to grow, to build up and to progress. Truth and trust are everywhere, all around you and as far as you can imagine, perceive or see. The plants are joyously growing and producing the good things of life. Disease free fruits and vegetables are plentiful and ready to provide you with the substances of a healthy breakfast, lunch and dinner. You take a deep breath of a clean earthly atmosphere, smile, laugh, love and enjoy. Life is so good, so much better than before the change. You are free. No more exploitation of your life and services to feed the appetites of a few greedy and power hungry monsters. Making money on the destruction of the atmosphere, the world and the people in it has now deteriorated and crumbled into oblivion.

The very goal of money, power and manipulation have crumbled from the weight that it inadvertently placed upon its own sandy foundation. Its subscription to lies and deception for power and riches have vaporized and been done away with. Radiation from hot fusion and the pollution created by the burning of fossil fuels are no more. No more polluting the earth and human health for the sake of money, power and control of the masses. The possibilities are enormous and endless. Trust is all around. The rest is up to you.

In the Pollyanna Zone there are no poor people. Everyone is rich. They are rich, not by having more than they need but by having everything they need. When all things are shared, access to resources are not restricted by the lack of money. Is it orderly, yes, it is. Waste is limited by the free availability of information and advice, preventing a great deal of error. Product development is supported by the participation and enthusiasm of the entire society. There are no law suits, only discussion and conclusions are drawn on sensibility, not selfish manipulation. Any desire to gain an upper hand or for greater profits is immediately suppressed by the people. Is it socialism. no, it is charitable cooperation. Although there is a resemblance, yes but there is a key difference. The difference is a fine line. That fine line is charity.

If anyone seeks to have dominion over another, charity in that person is lost. That person no longer has the capacity to love any person the minute he seeks to have power and dominion over them. Power corrupts with the very first step. In a free society, dominion will be stopped at the outset because it cannot be tolerated in a true free society. It is impossible for people in any society to be free when anyone is allowed to have control and dominate another. Competition is not to dominate or gain an advantage over a neighbor but instead it is in cooperation with the neighbor and concentrated on challenging the obstacles and lack of understanding that stands in the way of progress and improvement. People rejoice in the accomplishments of others because they have learned that to do so raises themselves to a higher level of improvement, peace and satisfaction. Besides, everything belongs to everybody. It is not communism or socialism controlled by a mindless government, it is freedom and personal agency of the highest order, all regulated by common charity and love, shared by everyone.

You are now in the Pollyanna Zone, a true millennial dawning. Welcome! Charity and clean, healthy living are everywhere. All people share and trust one another. Integrity is the norm and the tradition of all people in the zone. Energy is free and there is pollution of neither human character nor the earth and the atmosphere. Without one, there cannot be the other. Can it be achieved, I hope so and I also think it is possible. Onward and upward, I say. Carry on and continue to personally improve. Of course it is not possible in the self aggrandizing attitudes in the world as we have come to know it but change is on the horizon. The future holds wonderful possibilities for clean air, clean, free energy, food production and distribution to all without the discriminating economics that starve the poor and line the pockets of a few rich individuals with a currency they cannot eat nor use to warm themselves. The Pollyanna Zone is true freedom of the highest order. Get ready, be as good as you know how to be, for it is coming and very soon.

www.ingramcontent.com/pod-product-compliance
Lightning Source LLC
Chambersburg PA
CBHW060017210326
41520CB00009B/921